P9-CMF-439

English Men of Letters

EDITED BY JOHN MORLEY

ROBERT BURNS

BY

PRINCIPAL SHAIRP

PROFESSOR OF POETRY IN THE UNIVERSITY OF OXFORD

NEW YORK

HARPER & BROTHERS, PUBLISHERS

FRANKLIN SQUARE

ENGLISH MEN OF LETTERS.

EDITED BY JOHN MORLEY.

JOHNSON	Leslie Stephen.	COWPER	Goldwin Smith.
GIBBON	J. C. Morison.	POPE	Leslie Stephen.
SCOTT	R. H. Hutton.	BYRON	John Nichol.
SHELLEY	J. A. Symonds.	LOCKE	Thomas Fowler.
HUME	T. H. Huxley.	WORDSWORTH	F. Myers.
GOLDSMITH	William Black.	DRYDEN	G. Saintsbury.
DEFOE	William Minto.	LANDOR	Sidney Colvin.
BURNS	J. C. Shairp.	DE QUINCEY	David Masson.
SPENSER	R. W. Church.	LAMB	Alfred Ainger.
THACKERAY	Anthony Trollope.	BENTLEY	R. C. Jebb.
BURKE	John Morley.	DICKENS	A. W. Ward.
MILTON	Mark Pattison.	GRAY	E. W. Gosse.
HAWTHORNE	Henry James, Jr.	SWIFT	Leslie Stephen.
SOUTHEY	E. Dowden.	STERNE	H. D. Traill.
CHAUCER	A. W. Ward.	MACAULAY	J. Cotter Morison.
BUNYAN	J. A. Froude.	FIELDING	Austin Dobson.
	SHERIDAN ... Mrs. Oliphant.		

12mo, Cloth, 75 cents per volume.

PUBLISHED BY HARPER & BROTHERS, NEW YORK.

☞ Any of the above works will be sent by mail, postage prepaid, to any part of the United States, on receipt of the price.

CONTENTS.

1339

ROBERT BURNS.

CHAPTER I.

YOUTH IN AYRSHIRE.

GREAT men, great events, great epochs, it has been said,
grow as we recede from them; and the rate at which they
grow in the estimation of men is in some sort a measure
of their greatness.   Tried by this standard, Burns must
be great indeed; for, during the eighty years that have
passed since his death, men's interest in the man himself
and their estimate of his genius have been steadily increasing.   Each decade since he died has produced at least
two biographies of him.   When Mr. Carlyle wrote his well-
known essay on Burns in 1828, he could already number
six biographies of the Poet, which had been given to the
world during the previous thirty years; and the interval
between 1828 and the present day has added, in at least
the same proportion, to their number.   What it was in the
man and in his circumstances that has attracted so much
of the world's interest to Burns, I must make one more
attempt to describe.

If success were that which most secures men's sympathy,
Burns would have won but little regard; for in all but his

poetry his was a defeated life—sad and heart-depressing to contemplate beyond the lives even of most poets.

Perhaps it may be the very fact that in him so much failure and shipwreck were combined with such splendid gifts, that has attracted to him so deep and compassionate interest. Let us review once more the facts of that life, and tell again its oft-told story.

It was on the 25th of January, 1759, about two miles from the town of Ayr, in a clay-built cottage, reared by his father's own hands, that Robert Burns was born. The " auld clay bigging " which saw his birth still stands by the side of the road that leads from Ayr to the river and the bridge of Doon. Between the banks of that romantic stream and the cottage is seen the roofless ruin of " Allo-way's auld haunted kirk," which Tam o' Shanter has made famous. His first welcome to the world was a rough one. As he himself says—

> " A blast o' Janwar' win'
> Blew hansel in on Robin."

A few days after his birth, a storm blew down the gable of the cottage, and the poet and his mother were carried in the dark morning to the shelter of a neighbour's roof, under which they remained till their own home was re-paired. In after-years he would often say, " No wonder that one ushered into the world amid such a tempest should be the victim of stormy passions." " It is hard to be born in Scotland," says the brilliant Parisian. Burns had many hardships to endure, but he never reckoned this to be one of them.

His father, William Burness or Burnes, for so he spelt his name, was a native not of Ayrshire, but of Kincardine-shire, where he had been reared on a farm belonging to the forfeited estate of the noble but attainted house of Keith-Marischal. Forced to migrate thence at the age of nineteen, he had travelled to Edinburgh, and finally settled in Ayrshire, and at the time when Robert, his eldest child, was born, he rented seven acres of land, near the Brig o' Doon, which he cultivated as a nursery-garden. He was a man of strict, even stubborn integrity, and of strong temper—a combination which, as his son remarks, does not usually lead to worldly success. But his chief characteristic was his deep-seated and thoughtful piety. A peasant-saint of the old Scottish stamp, he yet tempered the stern Calvinism of the West with the milder Arminianism more common in his northern birthplace. Robert, who, amid all his after-errors, never ceased to revere his father's memory, has left an immortal portrait of him in *The Cotter's Saturday Night*, when he describes how

"The saint, the father, and the husband prays."

William Burness was advanced in years before he married, and his wife, Agnes Brown, was much younger than himself. She is described as an Ayrshire lass, of humble birth, very sagacious, with bright eyes and intelligent looks, but not beautiful, of good manners and easy address. Like her husband, she was sincerely religious, but of a more equable temper, quick to perceive character, and with a memory stored with old traditions, songs, and ballads, which she told or sang to amuse her children. In his outer man the poet resembled his mother, but his great mental gifts, if inherited at all, must be traced to his father. Three places in Ayrshire, besides his birthplace, will always be remembered as the successive homes of Burns. These were Mount Oliphant, Lochlea (pronounced Lochly), and Mossgiel.

MOUNT OLIPHANT. — This was a small upland farm, about two miles from the Brig o' Doon, of a poor and hungry soil, belonging to Mr. Ferguson, of Doon-holm, who was also the landlord of William Burness' previous holding. Robert was in his seventh year when his father entered on this farm at Whitsuntide, 1766, and he had reached his eighteenth when the lease came to a close in 1777. All the years between these two dates were to the family of Burness one long sore battle with untoward circumstances, ending in defeat. If the hardest toil and severe self-denial could have procured success, they would not have failed. It was this period of his life which Robert afterwards described, as combining "the cheerless gloom of a hermit with the unceasing moil of galley-slave." The family did their best, but a niggard soil and bad seasons were too much for them. At length, on the death of his landlord, who had always dealt generously by him, William Burness fell into the grip of a factor, whose tender mercies were hard. This man wrote letters which set the whole family in tears. The poet has not given his name, but he has preserved his portrait in colours which are indelible :

> "I've noticed, on our Laird's court-day,
> An' mony a time my heart's been wae,
> Poor tenant bodies, scant o' cash,
> How they maun thole a factor's snash ;
> He'll stamp an' threaten, curse and swear,
> He'll apprehend them, poind their gear,
> While they maun stan', wi aspect humble,
> And hear it a', an' fear an' tremble."

In his autobiographical sketch the poet tells us that, "The farm proved a ruinous bargain. I was the eldest of seven children, and my father, worn out by early hardship, was unfit for labour. His spirit was soon irritated, but not easily broken. There was a freedom in the lease in two years more; and to weather these two years we retrenched expenses, and toiled on." Robert and Gilbert, the two eldest, though still boys, had to do each a grown man's full work. Yet, for all their hardships, these Mount Oliphant days were not without alleviations. If poverty was at the door, there was warm family affection by the fireside. If the two sons had, long before manhood, to bear toil beyond their years, still they were living under their parents' roof, and those parents two of the wisest and best of Scotland's peasantry. Work was no doubt incessant, but education was not neglected — rather it was held one of the most sacred duties. When Robert was five years old, he had been sent to a school at Alloway Mill; and when the family removed to Mount Oliphant, his father combined with four of his neighbours to hire a young teacher, who boarded among them, and taught their children for a small salary. This young teacher, whose name was Murdoch, has left an interesting description of his two young pupils, their parents, and the household life while he sojourned at Mount Oliphant. At that time Murdoch thought that Gilbert possessed a livelier imagination, and was more of a wit than Robert. "All the mirth and liveliness," he says, "were with Gilbert. Robert's countenance at that time wore generally a grave and thoughtful look." Had their teacher been then told that one of his two pupils would become a great poet, he would have fixed on Gilbert. When he tried to teach them church music along with other rustic lads, they two lagged far behind the rest. Robert's voice especially was untuneable, and his ear so dull that it was with difficulty he could distinguish one tune from another. Yet this was he

who was to become the greatest song-writer that Scotland
—perhaps the world—has known. In other respects the
mental training of the lads was of the most thorough
kind. Murdoch taught them not only to read, but to
parse, and to give the exact meaning of the words, to turn
verse into the prose order, to supply ellipses, and to sub-
stitute plain for poetic words and phrases. How many of
our modern village schools even attempt as much! When
Murdoch gave up, the father himself undertook the education of his children, and carried it on at night after work-
hours were over. Of that father Murdoch speaks as by
far the best man he ever knew. Tender and affectionate
towards his children he describes him, seeking not to drive,
but to lead them to the right, by appealing to their conscience and their better feelings, rather than to their fears.
To his wife he was gentle and considerate in an unusual
degree, always thinking of her ease and comfort; and she
repaid it with the utmost reverence. She was a careful
and thrifty housewife; but, whenever her domestic tasks
allowed, she would return to hang with devout attention
on the discourse that fell from her wise husband. Under
that father's guidance knowledge was sought for as hid
treasure, and this search was based on the old and rever-
ential faith that increase of knowledge is increase of wisdom and goodness. The readings of the household were
wide, varied, and unceasing. Some one entering the house
at meal-time found the whole family seated, each with a
spoon in one hand and a book in the other. The books
which Burns mentions as forming part of their reading at
Mount Oliphant surprise us even now. Not only the ordinary school-books and geographies, not only the traditional life of Wallace, and other popular books of that sort,
but The Spectator, odd plays of Shakespeare, Pope (his

Homer included), Locke on the Human Understanding, Boyle's Lectures, Taylor's Scripture Doctrine of Original Sin, Allan Ramsay's works, formed the staple of their reading. Above all there was a collection of songs, of which Burns says, " This was my *vade mecum.* I pored over them driving my cart, or walking to labour, song by song, verse by verse; carefully noting the true, tender, or sublime, from affectation and fustian. I am convinced I owe to this practice much of my critic-craft, such as it is!" And he could not have learnt it in a better way.

There are few countries in the world which could at that time have produced in humble life such a teacher as Murdoch and such a father as William Burness. It seems fitting, then, that a country which could rear such men among its peasantry should give birth to such a poet as Robert Burns to represent them. The books which fed his young intellect were devoured only during intervals snatched from hard toil. That toil was no doubt excessive. And this early overstrain showed itself soon in the stoop of his shoulders, in nervous disorder about the heart, and in frequent fits of despondency. Yet perhaps too much has sometimes been made of these bodily hardships, as though Burns's boyhood had been one long misery. But the youth which grew up in so kindly an atmosphere of wisdom and home affection, under the eye of such a father and mother, cannot be called unblest.

Under the pressure of toil and the entire want of society, Burns might have grown up the rude and clownish and unpopular lad that he has been pictured in his early teens. But in his fifteenth summer there came to him a new influence, which at one touch unlocked the springs of new emotions. This incident must be given in his own words: " You know," he says, " our country custom of

coupling a man and woman together as partners in the labours of the harvest.   In my fifteenth summer my partner
was a bewitching creature, a year younger than myself.
My scarcity of English denies me the power of doing her
justice in that language, but you know the Scottish idiom.
She was a bonnie, sweet, sonsie lass.   In short, she, altogether unwittingly to herself, initiated me in that delicious
passion, which, in spite of acid disappointment, gin-horse
prudence, and book-worm philosophy, I hold to be the
first of human joys here below!   How she caught the
contagion I cannot tell. . . . Indeed, I did not know
myself why I liked so much to loiter behind with her,
when returning in the evening from our labours; why the
tones of her voice made my heartstrings thrill like an
Æolian harp; and especially why my pulse beat such a
furious ratan when I looked and fingered over her little
hand, to pick out the cruel nettle-stings and thistles.
Among her love-inspiring qualities, she sung sweetly; and
it was her favourite reel to which I attempted giving an
embodied vehicle in rhyme.   I was not so presumptuous
as to imagine that I could make verses like printed ones,
composed by men who read Greek and Latin; but my
girl sung a song which was said to be composed by a
country laird's son, on one of his father's maids, with
whom he was in love; and I saw no reason why I might
not rhyme as well as he; for, excepting that he could
shear sheep and cast peats, his father living in the moor-
lands, he had no more scholar-craft than myself.   Thus
with me began love and poetry."

The song he then composed is entitled "Handsome
Nell," and is the first he ever wrote.   He himself speaks
of it as very puerile and silly—a verdict which Chambers
endorses, but in which I cannot agree.   Simple and artless

it no doubt is, but with a touch of that grace which be-speaks the true poet. Here is one verse which, for direct-ness of feeling and felicity of language, he hardly ever surpassed:

> " She dresses aye sae clean and neat,
>   Baith decent and genteel,
> And then there's something in her gait
>   Gars ony dress look weel."

" I composed it," says Burns, "in a wild enthusiasm of passion, and to this hour I never recollect it but my heart melts, my blood sallies at the remembrance."

LOCHLEA.—Escaped from the fangs of the factor, with some remnant of means, William Burness removed from Mount Oliphant to Lochlea, in the parish of Tarbolton (1777); an upland, undulating farm, on the north bank of the River Ayr, with a wide outlook, southward over the hills of Carrick, westward toward the Isle of Arran, Ailsa Craig, and down the Firth of Clyde, toward the Western Sea. This was the home of Burns and his family from his eighteenth till his twenty-fifth year. For a time the family life here was more comfortable than before, proba-bly because several of the children were now able to assist their parents in farm labour. "These seven years," says Gilbert Burns, "brought small literary improvement to Robert"—but I can hardly believe this, when we remember that Lochlea saw the composition of *The Death and Dying Words of Poor Mailie*, and of *My Nannie, O*, and one or two more of his most popular songs. It was during those days that Robert, then growing into manhood, first vent-ured to step beyond the range of his father's control, and to trust the promptings of his own social instincts and headlong passions. The first step in this direction was to go to a dancing-school, in a neighbouring village, that he might there meet companions of either sex, and give his rustic manners " a brush," as he phrases it. The next step was taken when Burns resolved to spend his nineteenth summer in Kirkoswald, to learn mensuration and surveying from the schoolmaster there, who was famous as a teacher of these things. Kirkoswald, on the Carrick coast, was a village full of smugglers and adventurers, in whose society Burns was introduced to scenes of what he calls "swaggering riot and roaring dissipation." It may readily be believed that, with his strong love of sociality and excitement, he was an apt pupil in that school. Still the mensuration went on, till one day, when in the kail-yard behind the teacher's house, Burns met a young lass, who set his heart on fire, and put an end to mensuration. This incident is celebrated in the song beginning—

> "Now westlin winds and slaughtering guns
>   Bring autumn's pleasant weather "—

" the ebullition," he calls it, " of that passion which ended the school business at Kirkoswald."

From this time on for several years, love-making was his chief amusement, or rather his most serious business. His brother tells us that he was in the secret of half the love affairs of the parish of Tarbolton, and was never without at least one of his own. There was not a comely girl in Tarbolton on whom he did not compose a song, and then he made one which included them all. When he was thus inly moved, "the agitations of his mind and body," says Gilbert, "exceeded anything of the kind I ever knew in real life. He had always a particular jealousy of people who were richer than himself, or had more consequence. His love, therefore, rarely settled on persons of this description." The jealousy here noted, as extending even to his loves, was one of the weakest points of the poet's character. Of the ditties of that time, most of which have been preserved, the best specimen is *My Nannie, O.* This song, and the one entitled *Mary Morison,* render the whole scenery and sentiment of those rural meetings in a manner at once graphic and free from coarseness. Yet, truth to speak, it must be said that those gloamin' trysts, however they may touch the imagination and lend themselves to song, do in reality lie at the root of much that degrades the life and habits of the Scottish peasantry.

But those first three or four years at Lochlea, if not free from peril, were still with the poet times of innocence. His brother Gilbert, in the words of Chambers, "used to speak of his brother as at this period, to himself, a more admirable being than at any other. He recalled with delight the days when they had to go with one or two companions to cut peats for the winter fuel; because Robert was sure to enliven their toil with a rattling fire of witty remarks on men and things, mingled with the expressions of a genial, glowing heart, and the whole perfectly free from the taint which he afterwards acquired from his contact with the world. Not even in those volumes which afterwards charmed his country from end to end, did Gilbert see his brother in so interesting a light as in these conversations in the bog, with only two or three noteless peasants for an audience."

While Gilbert acknowledges that his brother's love-makings were at this time unceasing, he asserts that they were "governed by the strictest rules of virtue and modesty, from which he never deviated till he reached his twenty-third year." It was towards the close of his twenty-second that there occurs the record of his first serious desire to marry and settle in life. He had set his affections on a young woman named Ellison Begbie, daughter of a small farmer, and at that time servant in a family on Cessnock Water, about two miles from Lochlea. She is said to have been not a beauty, but of unusual liveliness and grace of mind. Long afterwards, when he had seen much of the world, Burns spoke of this young woman as, of all those on whom he ever fixed his fickle affections, the one most likely to have made a pleasant partner for life. Four letters which he wrote to her are preserved, in which he expresses the most pure and honourable feelings in language which, if a little formal, is, for manliness and simplicity, a striking contrast to the bombast of some of his later epistles. Songs, too, he addressed to her—*The Lass of Cessnock Banks*, *Bonnie Peggy Alison*, and *Mary Morison*. The two former are inconsiderable; the latter is one of those pure and beautiful love-lyrics, in the manner of the old ballads, which, as Hazlitt says, "take the deepest and most lasting hold on the mind."

"Yestreen, when to the trembling string,
    The dance gaed thro' the lighted ha',
To thee my fancy took its wing,
    I sat, but neither heard nor saw:
Tho' this was fair, and that was braw,
    And yon the toast of a' the town,
I sigh'd, and said amang them a',
    'Ye are na Mary Morison.'"

"Oh, Mary, canst thou wreck his peace,
    Wha for thy sake wad gladly die;
Or canst thou break that heart of his,
    Whase only faut is loving thee?
If love for love thou wilt na gie,
    At least be pity to me shown;

A thought ungentle canna be
  The thought o' Mary Morison."

In these lines the lyric genius of Burns was for the first
time undeniably revealed.

But neither letters nor love-songs prevailed. The
young woman, for some reason untold, was deaf to his
entreaties; and the rejection of this his best affection fell
on him with a malign influence, just as he was setting his
face to learn a trade which he hoped would enable him to
maintain a wife.

Irvine was at that time a centre of the flax-dressing art,
and as Robert and his brother raised flax on their farm,
they hoped that if they could dress as well as grow flax,
they might thereby double their profits. As he met with
this heavy disappointment in love just as he was setting
out for Irvine, he went thither down-hearted and depressed, at Midsummer, 1781. All who met him at that time
were struck with his look of melancholy, and his moody
silence, from which he roused himself only when in pleasant female society, or when he met with men of intelli-
gence. But the persons of this sort whom he met in Irvine were probably few. More numerous were the smugglers and rough-living adventurers with which that seaport
town, as Kirkoswald, swarmed. Among these he contracted, says Gilbert, "some acquaintance of a freer manner of thinking and living than he had been used to,
whose society prepared him for overleaping the bonds of
rigid virtue which had hitherto restrained him." One
companion, a sailor-lad of wild life and loose and irregular habits, had a wonderful fascination for Burns, who admired him for what he thought his independence and
magnanimity. "He was," says Burns, "the only man I
ever knew who was a greater fool than myself, where

woman was the presiding star; but he spoke of lawless
love with levity, which hitherto I had regarded with hor-
ror. *Here his friendship did me a mischief.*"

Another companion, older than himself, thinking that
the religious views of Burns were too rigid and uncompro-
mising, induced him to adopt "more liberal opinions,"
which in this case, as in so many others, meant more lax
opinions. With his principles of belief, and his rules of
conduct at once assailed and undermined, what chart or
compass remained any more for a passionate being like
Burns over the passion-swept sea of life that lay before
him? The migration to Irvine was to him the descent to
Avernus, from which he never afterwards, in the actual
conduct of life, however often in his hours of inspiration,
escaped to breathe again the pure upper air. This brief
but disastrous Irvine sojourn was brought to a sudden
close. Burns was robbed by his partner in trade, his flax-
dressing shop was burnt to the ground by fire during the
carousal of a New-Year's morning, and himself, impaired
in purse, in spirits, and in character, returned to Lochlea
to find misfortunes thickening round his family, and his
father on his death-bed. For the old man, his long struggle with scanty means, barren soil, and bad seasons, was
now near its close. Consumption had set in. Early in
1784, when his last hour drew on, the father said that
there was one of his children of whose future he could not
think without fear. Robert, who was in the room, came
up to his bedside and asked, "O father, is it me you
mean?" The old man said it was. Robert turned to the
window, with tears streaming down his cheeks, and his
bosom swelling, from the restraint he put on himself, almost to bursting. The father had early perceived the genius that was in his boy, and even in Mount Oliphant days

had said to his wife, "Whoever lives to see it, something extraordinary will come from that boy." He had lived to see and admire his son's earliest poetic efforts. But he had also noted the strong passions, with the weak will, which might drive him on the shoals of life.

MOSSGIEL.—Towards the close of 1783, Robert and his brother, seeing clearly the crash of family affairs which was impending, had taken on their own account a lease of the small farm of Mossgiel, about two or three miles distant from Lochlea, in the parish of Mauchline. When their father died in February, 1784, it was only by claiming the arrears of wages due to them, and ranking among their father's creditors, that they saved enough from the domestic wreck to stock their new farm. Thither they conveyed their widowed mother, and their younger brothers and sisters, in March, 1784. Their new home was a bare, upland farm, 118 acres of cold clay soil, lying within a mile of Mauchline village. Burns entered on it with a firm resolution to be prudent, industrious, and thrifty. In his own words, "I read farming books, I calculated crops, I attended markets, and, in short, in spite of the devil, the world, and the flesh, I should have been a wise man; but the first year, from unfortunately buying bad seed—the second, from a late harvest, we lost half our crops. This overset all my wisdom, and I returned like the dog to his vomit, and the sow that was washed to her wallowing in the mire." Burns was in the beginning of his twenty-sixth year when he took up his abode at Mossgiel, where he remained for four years. Three things those years and that bare moorland farm witnessed—the wreck of his hopes as a farmer, the revelation of his genius as a poet, and the frailty of his character as a man. The result of the immoral habits and "liberal opinions" which he had

learnt at Irvine were soon apparent in that event of which
he speaks in his *Epistle to John Rankine* with such unbe-
coming levity.   In the Chronological Edition of his works
it is painful to read on one page the pathetic lines which
he engraved on his father's headstone, and a few pages on,
written almost at the same time, the epistle above alluded
to, and other poems in the same strain, in which the defiant poet glories in his shame.   It was well for the old
man that he was laid in Alloway Kirkyard before these
things befell.   But the widowed mother had to bear the
burden, and to receive in her home and bring up the child
that should not have been born.   When silence and shame
would have most become him, Burns poured forth his feelings in ribald verses, and bitterly satirized the parish minister, who required him to undergo that public penance
which the discipline of the Church at that time exacted.
Whether this was a wise discipline or not, no blame attached to the minister, who merely carried out the rules
which his Church enjoined.   It was no proof of magnanimity in Burns to use his talent in reviling the minister,
who had done nothing more than his duty.   One can
hardly doubt but that in his inmost heart he must have
been visited with other and more penitential feelings than
those unseemly verses express.   But, as Lockhart has well
observed, "his false pride recoiled from letting his jovial
associates know how little he was able to drown the whispers of the still small voice ; and the fermenting bitterness
of a mind ill at ease within himself escaped—as may be
often traced in the history of satirists—in angry sarcasms
against those who, whatever their private errors might be,
had at least done him no wrong."   Mr. Carlyle's comment
on this crisis of his life is too weighty to be omitted here.
With principles assailed by evil example from without,

by 'passions raging like demons' from within, he had little need of sceptical misgivings to whisper treason in the
heat of the battle, or to cut off his retreat if he were already defeated. He loses his feeling of innocence; his
mind is at variance with itself; the old divinity no longer
presides there; but wild Desires and wild Repentance al-
ternately oppress him. Ere long, too, he has committed
himself before the world; his character for sobriety, dear
to a Scottish peasant as few corrupted worldlings can even
conceive, is destroyed in the eyes of men; and his only
refuge consists in trying to disbelieve his guiltiness, and
is but a refuge of lies. The blackest desperation gathers
over him, broken only by the red lightnings of remorse."
Amid this trouble it was but a poor vanity and miserable love of notoriety which could console itself with the
thought—

> "The mair they talk, I'm kent the better,
>   E'en let them clash."

Or was this not vanity at all, but the bitter irony of self-
reproach?

This collision with the minister and Kirk Session of his
parish, and the bitter feelings it engendered in his rebellious
bosom, at once launched Burns into the troubled sea of religious controversy that was at that time raging all around
him. The clergy of the West were divided into two parties, known as the Auld Lights and the New Lights. Ayrshire and the west of Scotland had long been the strong-
hold of Presbyterianism and of the Covenanting spirit;
and in Burns's day—a century and a half after the Cove-
nant—a large number of the ministers still adhered to its
principles, and preached the Puritan theology undiluted.
These men were democratic in their ecclesiastical views,
and stout protesters against Patronage, which has always

been the bugbear of the sects in Scotland. As Burns expresses it, they did their best to stir up their flocks to

> " Join their counsel and their skills
>   To cowe the lairds,
> An' get the brutes the power themsels
>   To chuse their herds."

All Burns's instincts would naturally have been on the side of those who wished to resist patronage and " to cowe the lairds," had not this his natural tendency been counteracted by a stronger bias drawing him in an opposite direction. The Auld Lights, though democrats in Church politics, were the upholders of that strict Church discipline under which he was smarting, and to this party belonged his own minister, who had brought that discipline to bear upon him. Burns, therefore, naturally threw himself into the arms of the opposite, or New Light party, who were more easy in their life and in their doctrine. This large and growing section of ministers were deeply imbued with rationalism, or, as they then called it, " common-sense," in the light of which they pared away from religion all that was mysterious and supernatural. Some of them were said to be Socinians or even pure Deists, most of them shone less in the pulpit than at the festive board. With such men a person in Burns's then state of mind would readily sympathize, and they received him with open arms. Nothing could have been more unfortunate than that in this crisis of his career he should have fallen into intimacy with those hard-headed but coarse-minded men. They were the first persons of any pretensions to scholarly education with whom he had mingled freely. He amused them with the sallies of his wit and sarcasm, and astonished them by his keen insight and vigorous powers of rea-

soning. They abetted those very tendencies in his nature which required to be checked. Their countenance, as
clergymen, would allay the scruples and misgivings he
might otherwise have felt, and stimulate to still wilder
recklessness whatever profanity he might be tempted to
indulge in. When he had let loose his first shafts of satire against their stricter brethren, those New Light ministers heartily applauded him; and hounded him on to still
more daring assaults. He had not only his own quarrel
with his parish minister and the stricter clergy to revenge,
but the quarrel also of his friend and landlord, Gavin
Hamilton, a county lawyer, who had fallen under Church
censure for neglect of Church ordinances, and had been
debarred from the Communion. Burns espoused Gavin's
cause with characteristic zeal, and let fly new arrows one
after another from his satirical quiver.

The first of these satires against the orthodox ministers
was *The Twa Herds, or the Holy Tulzie,* written on a
quarrel between two brother clergymen. Then followed
in quick succession *Holy Willie's Prayer, The Ordination,*
and *The Holy Fair.* His good mother and his brother
were pained by these performances, and remonstrated
against them. But Burns, though he generally gave ear
to their counsel, in this instance turned a deaf ear to it,
and listened to other advisers. The love of exercising his
strong powers of satire and the applause of his boon-companions, lay and clerical, prevailed over the whispers of his
own better nature and the advice of his truest friends.
Whatever may be urged in defence of employing satire
to lash hypocrisy, I cannot but think that those who have
loved most what is best in Burns's poetry must have regretted that these poems were ever written. Some have
commended them on the ground that they have exposed

religious pretence and Pharisaism. The good they may have done in this way is perhaps doubtful. But the harm they have done in Scotland is not doubtful, in that they have connected in the minds of the people so many coarse and even profane thoughts with objects which they had regarded till then with reverence. Even *The Holy Fair*, the poem in this kind which is least offensive, turns on the abuses that then attended the celebration of the Holy Communion in rural parishes, and with great power portrays those gatherings in their most mundane aspects. Yet, as Lockhart has well remarked, those things were part of the same religious system which produced the scenes which Burns has so beautifully described in *The Cotter's Saturday Night*. Strange that the same mind, almost at the same moment, should have conceived two poems so different in spirit as *The Cotter's Saturday Night* and *The Holy Fair!*

I have dwelt thus long on these unpleasant satires that I may not have again to return to them. It is a more welcome task to turn to the other poems of the same period. Though Burns had entered on Mossgiel resolved to do his best as a farmer, he soon discovered that it was not in that way he was to attain success. The crops of 1784 and 1785 both failed, and their failure seems to have done something to drive him in on his own internal resources. He then for the first time seems to have awakened to the conviction that his destiny was to be a poet; and he forthwith set himself, with more resolution than he ever showed before or after, to fulfil that mission. Hitherto he had complained that his life had been without an aim; now he determined that it should be so no longer. The dawning hope began to gladden him that he might take his place among the bards of Scotland.

who, themselves mostly unknown, have created that atmosphere of minstrelsy which envelopes and glorifies their native country. This hope and aim is recorded in an entry of his commonplace book, of the probable date of August, 1784:

"However I am pleased with the works of our Scotch poets, particularly the excellent Ramsay, and the still more excellent Fergusson, yet I am hurt to see other places of Scotland, their towns, rivers, woods, and haughs, immortalized in such celebrated performances, while my dear native country — the ancient bailieries of Carrick, Kyle, and Cunningham, famous both in ancient and modern times for a gallant and warlike race of inhabitants — a country where civil, and particularly religious liberty, have ever found their first support, and their last asylum — a country, the birthplace of many famous philosophers, soldiers, and statesmen, and the scene of many important events recorded in Scottish history, particularly a great many of the actions of the glorious Wallace, the saviour of his country—yet we have never had one Scotch poet of any eminence to make the fertile banks of Irvine, the romantic woodlands and sequestered scenes of Ayr, and the heathy mountainous source and winding sweep of Doon, emulate Tay, Forth, Ettrick, Tweed. This is a complaint I would gladly remedy; but, alas! I am far unequal to the task, both in native genius and in education. Obscure I am, obscure I must be, though no young poet nor young soldier's heart ever beat more fondly for fame than mine."

Though the sentiment here expressed may seem commonplace and the language hardly grammatical, yet this extract clearly reveals the darling ambition that was now haunting the heart of Burns. It was the same wish

which he expressed better in rhyme at a later day in his
Epistle to the Gude Wife of Wauchope House.

> "E'en then, a wish, I mind its power,
>   A wish that to my latest hour
>   Shall strongly heave my breast,
>   That I for poor Auld Scotland's sake
>   Some usefu' plan or beuk could make,
>   Or sing a sang at least.
>   The rough burr-thistle, spreading wide
>   Amang the bearded bear,
>   I turn'd the weeder-clips aside,
>   An' spar'd the symbol dear."

It was about his twenty-fifth year when he first conceived the hope that he might become a national poet.
The failure of his first two harvests, 1784 and '85, in
Mossgiel, may well have strengthened this desire, and
changed it into a fixed purpose. If he was not to succeed as a farmer, might he not find success in another employment that was much more to his mind?

And this longing, so deeply cherished, he had, within
less than two years from the time that the above entry in
his diary was written, amply fulfilled. From the autumn
of 1784 till May, 1786, the fountains of poetry were un-
sealed within, and flowed forth in a continuous stream.
That period, so prolific of poetry that none like it ever
afterwards visited him, saw the production not only of
the satirical poems already noticed, and of another more
genial satire, *Death and Dr. Hornbook*, but also of those
characteristic epistles in which he reveals so much of his
own character, and of those other descriptive poems in
which he so wonderfully delineates the habits of the
Scottish peasantry.

Within from sixteen to eighteen months were composed, not only seven or eight long epistles to rhyme-composing brothers in the neighbourhood, David Sillar, John Lapraik, and others, but also, *Halloween, To a Mouse, The Jolly Beggars, The Cotter's Saturday Night, Address to the Deil, The Auld Farmer's Address to his Auld Mare, The Vision, The Twa Dogs, The Mountain Daisy.* The descriptive poems above named followed each other in rapid succession during that spring-time of his genius, having been all composed, as the latest edition of his works shows, in a period of about six months, between November, 1785, and April, 1786. Perhaps there are none of Burns's compositions which give the real man more naturally and unreservedly than his epistles. Written in the dialect he had learnt by his father's fireside, to friends in his own station, who shared his own tastes and feelings, they flow on in an easy stream of genial, happy spirits, in which kindly humour, wit, love of the outward world, knowledge of men, are all beautifully intertwined into one strand of poetry, unlike anything else that has been seen before or since. The outward form of the verse and the style of diction are no doubt after the manner of his two forerunners whom he so much admired, Ramsay and Fergusson; but the play of soul and power of expression, the natural grace with which they rise and fall, the vividness of every image, and transparent truthfulness of every sentiment, are all his own. If there is any exception to be made to this estimate, it is in the grudge which here and there peeps out against those whom he thought greater favourites of fortune than himself and his correspondents. But taken as a whole, I know not any poetic epistles to be compared with them. They are just the letters in which one friend might unbosom himself to another without the least artifice or disguise. And the broad Doric is so pithy, so powerful, so aptly fitted to the thought, that not even Horace himself has surpassed it in "curious felicity." Often when harvests were failing and the world going against him, he found his solace in pouring forth in rhyme his feelings to some trusted friend. As he says in one of these same epistles—

> "Leeze me on rhyme! it's aye a treasure,
> My chief, amaist my only pleasure,
> At hame, a-fiel', at wark, at leisure,
>   The Muse, poor hizzie!
> Tho' rough an' raploch be her measure,
>   She's seldom lazy."

Of the poems founded on the customs of the peasantry, I shall speak in the sequel. The garret in which all the poems of this period were written is thus described by Chambers: "The farmhouse of Mossgiel, which still exists almost unchanged since the days of the poet, is very small, consisting of only two rooms, a but and a ben, as they are called in Scotland. Over these, reached by a trap stair, is a small garret, in which Robert and his brother used to sleep. Thither, when he had returned from his day's work, the poet used to retire, and seat himself at a small deal table, lighted by a narrow skylight in the roof, to transcribe the verses which he had composed in the fields. His favourite time for composition was at the plough. Long years afterwards his sister, Mrs. Begg, used to tell how, when her brother had gone forth again to field-work, she would steal up to the garret and search the drawer of the deal table for the verses which Robert had newly transcribed."

In which of the poems of this period his genius is most conspicuous it might not be easy to determine. But there can be little question about the justice of Lockhart's remark, that "*The Cotter's Saturday Night* is of all Burns's pieces the one whose exclusion from the collection would be most injurious, if not to the genius of the poet, at least to the character of the man. In spite of many feeble lines, and some heavy stanzas, it appears to me that even his genius would suffer more in estimation by being contemplated in the absence of this poem, than of any other single poem he has left us." Certainly it is the one which has most endeared his name to the more thoughtful and earnest of his countrymen. Strange it is, not to say painful, to think that this poem, in which the simple and manly piety of his country is so finely touched, and the image of his own religious father so beautifully portrayed, should have come from the same hand which wrote nearly at the same time *The Jolly Beggars*, *The Ordination*, and *The Holy Fair*.

During those two years at Mossgiel, from 1784 to 1786, when the times were hard, and the farm unproductive, Burns must indeed have found poetry to be, as he himself says, its own reward. A nature like his required some vent for itself, some excitement to relieve the pressure of dull farm drudgery, and this was at once his purest and noblest excitement. In two other more hazardous forms of excitement he was by temperament disposed to seek refuge. These were conviviality and love-making. In the former of these, Gilbert says that he indulged little, if at all, during his Mossgiel period. And this seems proved by his brother's assertion that during all that time Robert's private expenditure never exceeded seven pounds a year. When he had dressed himself on this, and procured his other necessaries, the margin that remained for drinking must have been small indeed. But love-making—that had been with him, ever since he reached manhood, an un-

ceasing employment. Even in his later teens he had, as
his earliest songs show, given himself enthusiastically to
those nocturnal meetings, which were then and are still
customary among the peasantry of Scotland, and which at
the best are full of perilous temptation. But ever since
the time when, during his Irvine sojourn, he forsook the
paths of innocence, there is nothing in any of his love-af-
fairs which those who prize what was best in Burns would
not willingly forget. If here we allude to two such incidents, it is because they are too intimately bound up with
his life to be passed over in any account of it. Gilbert
says that while "one generally reigned paramount in Robert's affections, he was frequently encountering other at-
tractions, which formed so many underplots in the drama
of his love." This is only too evident in those two loves
which most closely touched his destiny at this time.

From the time of his settlement at Mossgiel frequent
allusions occur in his letters and poems to flirtations with
the belles of the neighbouring village of Mauchline.
 Among all these Jean Armour, the daughter of a respectable master-mason in that village, had the chief place in
his affections. All through 1785 their courtship had continued, but early in 1786 a secret and irregular marriage,
with a written acknowledgment of it, had to be effected.
Then followed the father's indignation that his daughter
should be married to so wild and worthless a man as
Burns; compulsion of his daughter to give up Burns, and
to destroy the document which vouched their marriage;
Burns's despair driving him to the verge of insanity; the
letting loose by the Armours of the terrors of the law
against him; his skulking for a time in concealment; his
resolve to emigrate to the West Indies, and become a
slave-driver. All these things were passing in the spring

months of 1786, and in September of the same year Jean
Armour became the mother of twin children.

It would be well if we might believe that the story of ✳
his betrothal to Highland Mary was, as Lockhart seems to
have thought, previous to and independent of the incidents
just mentioned.   But the more recent investigations of
Mr. Scott Douglas and Dr. Chambers have made it too
painfully clear that it was almost at the very time when
he was half distracted by Jean Armour's desertion of him,
and while he was writing his broken-hearted *Lament* over
her conduct, that there occurred, as an interlude, the episode of Mary Campbell.   This simple and sincere-hearted
girl from Argyllshire was, Lockhart says, the object of by
far the deepest passion Burns ever knew.   And Lockhart
gives at length the oft-told tale how, on the second Sunday of May, 1786, they met in a sequestered spot by the
banks of the River Ayr, to spend one day of parting love;
how they stood, one on either side of a small brook, laved
their hands in the stream, and, holding a Bible between
them, vowed eternal fidelity to each other.   They then
parted, never again to meet.   In October of the same year
Mary came from Argyllshire, as far as Greenock, in the
hope of meeting Burns, but she was there seized with a
malignant fever which soon laid her in an early grave.

The Bible, in two volumes, which Burns gave her on
that parting day, has been recently recovered.   On the
first volume is inscribed, in Burns's hand, " And ye shall
not swear by My Name falsely, I am the Lord.   Levit.
19th chap. 12th verse;" and on the second volume, " Thou
shalt not forswear thyself, but shalt perform unto the Lord
thine oath.   Matth. 5th chap. 33rd verse."   But the names
of Mary Campbell and Robert Burns, which were originally inscribed on the volumes, have been almost obliterated.

It has been suggested by Mr. Scott Douglas, the most recent editor who has investigated anew the whole incident, that, "in the whirl of excitement which soon followed that Sunday, Burns forgot his vow to poor Mary, and that she, heart-sore at his neglect, deleted the names from this touching memorial of their secret betrothal."

Certain it is that in the very next month, June, 1786, we find Burns, in writing to one of his friends about "poor, ill-advised, ungrateful Armour," declaring that, "to confess a truth between you and me, I do still love her to distraction after all, though I won't tell her so if I were to see her." And Chambers even suggests that there was still a third love interwoven, at this very time, in the complicated web of Burns's fickle affections. Burns, though he wrote several poems about Highland Mary, which afterwards appeared, never mentioned her name to any of his family. Even if there was no more in the story than what has been here given, no wonder that a heart like Burns, which, for all its unsteadfastness, never lost its sensibility, nor even a sense of conscience, should have been visited by the remorse which forms the burden of the lyric to Mary in heaven, written three years after.

> "Seest thou thy lover lowly laid?
> Hear'st thou the pangs that rend his breast?"

The misery of his condition, about the time when Highland Mary died, and the conflicting feelings which agitated him, are depicted in the following extract from a letter which he wrote probably about October, 1786, to his friend Robert Aiken:

"There are many things that plead strongly against it [seeking a place in the Excise]: the uncertainty of getting soon into business; the consequences of my follies, which

perhaps make it impracticable for me to stay at home;
and, besides, I have been for some time pining under secret wretchedness, from causes which you pretty well know
—the pang of disappointment, the sting of pride, with
some wandering stabs of remorse, which never fail to settle
on my vitals like vultures when attention is not called away
by the calls of society or the vagaries of the Muse.   Even
in the hour of social mirth, my gaiety is the madness of
an intoxicated criminal under the hands of the executioner.
All these reasons urge me to go abroad, and to all these
reasons I have only one answer—the feelings of a father.
This, in the present mood I am in, overbalances everything
that can be laid in the scale against it.   You may perhaps
think it an extravagant fancy, but it is a sentiment which
strikes home to my very soul; though sceptical in some
points of our current belief, yet I think I have every evidence for the reality of a life beyond the stinted bourne
of our present existence: if so, then how should I, in the
presence of that tremendous Being, the Author of existence, how should I meet the reproaches of those who stand
to me in the dear relation of children, whom I deserted in
the smiling innocency of helpless infancy? Oh, Thou great
unknown Power! Thou Almighty God! who hast lighted
up reason in my breast, and blessed me with immortality!
I have frequently wandered from that order and regularity
necessary for the perfection of Thy works, yet Thou hast
never left me nor forsaken me. . . ."

      *   *   *   *   *   *

"You see, sir, that if to know one's errors were a probability of mending them, I stand a fair chance; but, according to the reverend Westminster divines, though conviction must precede conversion, it is very far from always
implying it."

This letter exhibits the tumult of soul in which he had
been tossed during the last six months before it was written. He had by his own conduct wound round himself
complications from which he could not extricate himself,
yet which he could not but poignantly feel. One cannot
read of the "wandering stabs of remorse" of which he
speaks, without thinking of Highland Mary.

Some months before the above letter was written, in the
April of the same year, at the time when he first fell into
trouble with Jean Armour and her father, Burns had resolved to leave his country and sail for the West Indies.
He agreed with a Mr. Douglas to go to Jamaica and become a book-keeper on his estate there. But how were
funds to be got to pay his passage-money ? His friend
Gavin Hamilton suggested that the needed sum might be
raised, if he were to publish by subscription the poems he
had lying in his table-drawer.

Accordingly, in April, the publication of his poems was
resolved on. His friends, Gavin Hamilton of Mauchline,
Aiken and Ballantyne of Ayr, Muir and Parker of Kilmarnock, and others—all did their best to get the subscription
lists quickly filled. The last-named person put down his
own name for thirty-five copies. The printing of them
was committed to John Wilson, a printer in Kilmarnock,
and during May, June, and July of 1786, the work of the
press was going forward. In the interval between the resolution to publish and the appearance of the poems, during
his distraction about Jean Armour's conduct, followed by
the episode of Highland Mary, Burns gave vent to his own
dark feelings in some of the saddest strains that ever fell
from him—the lines on *The Mountain Daisy*, *The Lament*,
the Odes to *Despondency* and to *Ruin*. And yet so various were his moods, so versatile his powers, that it was

during that same interval that he composed, in a very different vein, *The Twa Dogs*, and probably also his satire of *The Holy Fair*. The following is the account the poet gives of these transactions in the autobiographical sketch of himself which he communicated to Dr. Moore:

"I now began to be known in the neighbourhood as a maker of rhyme. The first of my poetic offspring that saw light was a burlesque lamentation of a quarrel between two reverend Calvinists; both of them were *dramatis personæ* in my *Holy Fair*. I had a notion myself that the piece had some merit; but to prevent the worst, I gave a copy of it to a friend who was fond of such things, and told him that I could not guess who was the author of it, but that I thought it pretty clever. With a certain description of the clergy, as well as the laity, it met with a roar of applause.

"*Holy Willie's Prayer* next made its appearance, and alarmed the Kirk Session so much, that they held several meetings to look over their spiritual artillery, if haply any of it might be pointed against profane rhymers. Unluckily for me, my wandering led me on another side, within point-blank shot of their heaviest metal. This is the unfortunate incident which gave rise to my printed poem, *The Lament*. This was a most melancholy affair, which I cannot yet bear to reflect on, and had very nearly given me one or two of the principal qualifications for a place among those who have lost the chart and mistaken the reckoning of Rationality.

"I gave up my part of the farm to my brother, and made what little preparation was in my power for Jamaica. But, before leaving my native country for ever, I resolved to publish my poems. I weighed my productions as impartially as was in my power; I thought they had merit;

and it was a delicious idea that I should be called a clever
fellow, even though it should never reach my ears—a poor
negro-driver, or perhaps a victim to that inhospitable clime,
and gone to the world of spirits! I can truly say, that
pauvre inconnu as I then was, I had pretty nearly as high
an idea of my works as I have at this moment, when the
public has decided in their favour. . . .

"I threw off about six hundred copies, of which I got
subscriptions for about three hundred and fifty. My vanity was highly gratified by the reception I met with from
the public; and besides, I pocketed, all expenses deducted,
nearly twenty pounds. This sum came very seasonably, as
I was thinking of indenting myself, for want of money, to
procure a passage. As soon as I was master of nine guineas, the price of wafting me to the torrid zone, I took a
steerage passage in the first ship that was to sail from the
Clyde, for

'Hungry ruin had me in the wind.'

"I had been for some days skulking from covert to
covert, under all the terrors of a jail, as some ill-advised
people had uncoupled the merciless pack of the law at my
heels. I had taken the last farewell of my friends; my
chest was on the way to Greenock; I had composed the
last song I should ever measure in Caledonia, '*The gloomy
night is gathering fast*,' when a letter from Dr. Blackwood
to a friend of mine overthrew all my schemes, by opening
up new prospects to my poetic ambition."

It was at the close of July, while Burns was, according
to his own account, "wandering from one friend's house
to another," to avoid the jail with which he was threatened
by Jean Armour's father, that the volume appeared, con-
taining the immortal poems (1786). That Burns himself
had some true estimate of their real worth is shown by

the way in which he expresses himself in his preface to his volume.

Ushered in with what Lockhart calls a "modest and manly preface," the Kilmarnock volume went forth to the world. The fame of it spread at once like wild-fire throughout Ayrshire and the parts adjacent. This is the account of its reception given by Robert Heron, a young literary man, who was at that time living in the Stewartry of Kirkcudbright:—"Old and young, high and low, grave and gay, learned or ignorant, were alike delighted, agitated, transported. I was at that time resident in Galloway, contiguous to Ayrshire, and I can well remember how even ploughboys and maid-servants would have gladly bestowed the wages they earned most hardly, and which they wanted to purchase necessary clothing, if they might procure the works of Burns." The edition consisted of six hundred copies—three hundred and fifty had been subscribed for before publication, and the remainder seems to have been sold off in about two months from their first appearance. When all expenses were paid, Burns received twenty pounds as his share of the profits. Small as this sum was, it would have more than sufficed to convey him to the West Indies; and, accordingly, with nine pounds of it he took a steerage passage in a vessel which was expected to sail from Greenock at the beginning of September. But from one cause or another the day of sailing was postponed, his friends began to talk of trying to get him a place in the Excise, his fame was rapidly widening in his own country, and his powers were finding a response in minds superior to any which he had hitherto known. Up to this time he had not associated with any persons of a higher grade than the convivial lawyers of Mauchline and Ayr, and the mundane ministers of the New Light school. But now persons of every rank were anxious to become acquainted with the wonderful Ayrshire Ploughman, for it was by that name he now began to be known, just as in the next generation another poet of as humble birth was spoken of as The Ettrick Shepherd. The first persons of a higher order who sought the acquaintanceship of Burns were Dugald Stewart and Mrs. Dunlop of Dunlop. The former of these two was the celebrated Scotch metaphysician, one of the chief ornaments of Edinburgh and its University at the close of last and the beginning of this century. He happened to be passing the summer at Catrine, on the Ayr, a few miles from Burns's farm, and having been made acquainted with the poet's works and character by Mr. Mackenzie, the surgeon of Mauchline, he invited the poet and the medical man to dine with him at Catrine. The day of this meeting was the 23rd of October, only three days after that on which Highland Mary died. Burns met on that day not only the professor and his accomplished wife, but for the first time in his life dined with a live lord—a young nobleman, said to have been of high promise, Lord Daer, eldest son of the then Earl of Selkirk. He had been a former pupil of Dugald Stewart, and happened to be at that time his guest. Burns has left the following humorous record of his own feelings at that meeting :

> "This wot ye all whom it concerns,
>   I, Rhymer Robin, alias Burns,
>   October twenty-third,
>   A ne'er to be forgotten day,
>   Sae far I sprachled up the brae [clambered],
>   I dinner'd wi' a Lord.
> *   *   *   *   *   *
> "But wi' a Lord ! stand out my shin,
>   A Lord—a Peer, an Earl's Son !

Up higher yet my bonnet !
And sic a Lord ! lang Scotch ells twa,
Our Peerage he o'erlooks them a',
        As I look o'er a sonnet.

"But oh for Hogarth's magic power !
To show Sir Bardie's willyart glower [bewildered],
        And how he stared and stammered,
When goavan, as if led in branks [moving stupidly],
And stumpin' on his ploughman shanks,
        He in the parlour hammered.

"I sidling sheltered in a nook,
An' at his Lordship steal't a look
        Like some portentous omen;
Except good sense and social glee,
An' (what surprised me) modesty,
        I markèd nought uncommon.

"I watched the symptoms o' the great,
The gentle pride, the lordly state,
        The arrogant assuming;
The fient a pride, nae pride had he,
Nor sauce, nor state, that I could see,
        Mair than an honest ploughman."

From this record of that evening given by Burns, it is
interesting to turn to the impression made on Professor
Stewart by this their first interview.   He says:

"His manners were then, as they continued ever afterwards, simple, manly, and independent; strongly expressive of conscious genius and worth, but without anything
that indicated forwardness, arrogance, or vanity.   He took
his share in conversation, but not more than belonged to
him; and listened with apparent attention and deference
on subjects where his want of education deprived him of
the means of information.   If there had been a little more
of gentleness and accommodation in his temper, he would,

I think, have been still more interesting; but he had been
accustomed to give law in the circle of his ordinary acquaintance, and his dread of anything approaching to
meanness or servility rendered his manner somewhat decided and hard.   Nothing, perhaps, was more remarkable
among his various attainments than the fluency, and pre-
cision, and originality of his language, when he spoke in
company; more particularly as he aimed at purity in his
turn of expression, and avoided, more successfully than
most Scotchmen, the peculiarities of Scottish phraseology."

Burns parted with Dugald Stewart, after this evening
spent with him in Ayrshire, to meet him again in the
Edinburgh coteries, amid which the professor shone as a
chief light.

Not less important in the history of Burns was his first
introduction to Mrs. Dunlop of Dunlop, a lady who continued the constant friend of himself and of his family
while she lived.   She was said to be a lineal descendant
of the brother of the great hero of Scotland, William Wallace.   Gilbert Burns gives the following account of the
way in which his brother's acquaintance with this lady
began:

"Of all the friendships, which Robert acquired in Ayrshire or elsewhere, none seemed more agreeable to him
than that of Mrs. Dunlop of Dunlop, nor any which has
been more uniformly and constantly exerted in behalf of
him and his family, of which, were it proper, I could give
many instances.   Robert was on the point of setting out
for Edinburgh before Mrs. Dunlop heard of him.   About
the time of my brother's publishing in Kilmarnock, she
had been afflicted with a long and severe illness, which had
reduced her mind to the most distressing state of depression.   In this situation, a copy of the printed poems was

laid on her table by a friend; and happening to open on
The Cotter's Saturday Night, she read it over with the
greatest pleasure and surprise; the poet's description of
the simple cottagers operating on her mind like the charm
of a powerful exorcist, expelling the demon *ennui*, and re-
storing her to her wonted inward harmony and satisfaction. Mrs. Dunlop sent off a person express to Mossgiel,
distant fifteen or sixteen miles, with a very obliging letter
to my brother, desiring him to send her half a dozen copies of his poems, if he had them to spare, and begging he
would do her the pleasure of calling at Dunlop House as
soon as convenient. This was the beginning of a correspondence which ended only with the poet's life. Nearly
the last use he made with his pen was writing a short letter to this lady a few days before his death."

The success of the first edition of his poems naturally
made Burns anxious to see a second edition begun. He
applied to his Kilmarnock printer, who refused the venture, unless Burns could supply ready money to pay for
the printing. This he could not do. But the poems by
this time had been read and admired by the most cultivated men in Edinburgh, and more than one word of en-
couragement had reached him from that city. The earliest of these was contained in a letter from the blind poet,
Dr. Blacklock, to whom Mr. Laurie, the kindly and accomplished minister of Loudoun, had sent the volume. This
Mr. Laurie belonged to the more cultivated section of the
Moderate party in the Church, as it was called, and was
the friend of Dr. Hugh Blair, Principal Robertson, and
Dr. Blacklock, and had been the channel through which
Macpherson's fragments of Ossian had first been brought
under the notice of that literary circle, which afterwards
introduced them to the world. The same worthy minister

had, on the first appearance of the poems, made Burns's
acquaintance, and had received him with warm-hearted
hospitality. This kindness the poet acknowledged, on one
of his visits to the Manse of Loudoun, by leaving in the
room in which he slept a short poem of six very feeling
stanzas, which contained a prayer for the family. This is
the last stanza—

> " When soon or late they reach that coast,
>   O'er life's rough ocean driven,
> May they rejoice, no wanderer lost,
>   A family in heaven !"

As soon as Mr. Laurie received the letter from Dr. Blacklock, written on the 4th September, in which warm admiration of the Kilmarnock volume was expressed, he forwarded it to Burns at Mossgiel. The result of it fell like
sunshine on the young poet's heart; for, as he says, "The
doctor belonged to a set of critics for whose applause I
had not dared to hope." The next word of approval from
Edinburgh was a highly appreciative criticism of the poems, which appeared in a number of *The Edinburgh Mag-
azine* at the beginning of November. Up till this time
Burns had not abandoned his resolution to emigrate to the
West Indies. But the refusal of the Kilmarnock printer
to undertake a new edition, and the voices of encourage-
ment reaching him from Edinburgh, combining with his
natural desire to remain, and be known as a poet, in his
native country, at length made him abandon the thought
of exile. On the 18th November we find him writing to
a friend, that he had determined on Monday or Tuesday,
the 27th or 28th November, to set his face toward the
Scottish capital and try his fortune there.

At this stage of the poet's career, Chambers pauses to
speculate on the feelings with which the humble family at

Mossgiel would hear of the sudden blaze of their brother's fame, and of the change it had made in his prospects. They rejoiced, no doubt, that he was thus rescued from compulsory banishment, and were no way surprised that the powers they had long known him to· possess had at length won the world's admiration. If he had fallen into evil courses, none knew it so well as they, and none had suffered more by these aberrations. Still, with all his faults, he had always been to them a kind son and brother, not loved the less for the anxieties he had caused them. But the pride and satisfaction they felt in his newly-won fame would be deep, not demonstrative. For the Burns family were a shy, reserved race, and like so many of the Scottish peasantry, the more they felt, the less they would express. In this they were very unlike the poet, with whom to have a feeling and to express it were almost synonymous. His mother, though not lacking in admiration of her son, is said to have been chiefly concerned lest the praises of his genius should make him forget the Giver of it. Such may have been the feelings of the poet's family.

What may we imagine his own feeling to have been in this crisis of his fate? The thought of Edinburgh society would naturally stir that ambition which was strong within him, and awaken a desire to meet the men who were praising him in the capital, and to try his powers in that wider arena. It might be that in that new scene something might occur which would reverse the current of his fortunes, and set him free from the crushing poverty that had hitherto kept him down. Anyhow, he was conscious of strong powers, which fitted him to shine, not in poetry only, but in conversation and discussion; and, ploughman though he was, he did not shrink from encountering any man or any set of men. Proud, too, we know he was, and

his pride often showed itself in jealousy and suspicion of
the classes who were socially above him, until such feelings were melted by kindly intercourse with some individual man belonging to the suspected orders.   He felt himself to surpass in natural powers those who were his superiors in rank and fortune, and he could not, for the life
of him, see why they should be full of this world's goods,
while he had none of them.   He had not yet learned—he
never did learn — that lesson, that the genius he had received was his allotted and sufficient portion, and that his
wisdom lay in making the most of this rare inward gift,
even on a meagre allowance of the world's external goods.
But perhaps, whether he knew it or not, the greatest at-
traction of the capital was the secret hope that in that
new excitement he might escape from the demons of remorse and despair which had for many months been dog-
ging him.   He may have fancied this, but the pangs which
Burns had created for himself were too deep to be in this
way permanently put by.

The secret of his settled unhappiness lay in the affections that he had abused in himself and in others who had
trusted him.   The course he had run since his Irvine sojourn was not of a kind to give peace to him or to any
man.   A coarse man of the world might have stifled the
tender voices that were reproaching him, and have gone on
his way uncaring that his conduct—

> "Hardened a' within,
> And petrified the feeling."

But Burns could not do this.   The heart that had responded so feelingly to the sufferings of lower creatures, the
unhoused mouse, the shivering cattle, the wounded hare,
could not without shame remember the wrongs he had

done to those human beings whose chief fault was that they had trusted him not wisely but too well. And these suggestions of a sensitive heart, conscience was at hand to enforce—a conscience wonderfully clear to discern the right, even when the will was least able to fulfil it. The excitements of a great city, and the loud praises of his fellow-men, might enable him momentarily to forget, but could not permanently stifle inward voices like these. So it was with a heart but ill at ease, bearing dark secrets he could tell to no one, that Burns passed from his Ayrshire cottage into the applause of the Scottish capital.

3

CHAPTER II.

THE journey of Burns from Mossgiel to Edinburgh was a sort of triumphal progress. He rode on a pony, lent him by a friend, and as the journey took two days, his resting-place the first night was at the farm-house of Covington Mains, in Lanarkshire, hard by the Clyde. The tenant of this farm, Mr. Prentice, was an enthusiastic admirer of Burns's poems, and had subscribed for twenty copies of the second edition. His son, years afterwards, in a letter to Christopher North, thus describes the evening on which Burns appeared at his father's farm:—"All the farmers in the parish had read the poet's then published works, and were anxious to see him. They were all asked to meet him at a late dinner, and the signal of his arrival was to be a white sheet attached to a pitchfork, and put on the top of a corn-stack in the barn-yard. The parish is a beautiful amphitheatre, with the Clyde winding through it—Wellbrae Hill to the west, Tinto Hill and the Culter Fells to the south, and the pretty, green, conical hill, Quothquan Law, to the east. My father's stack-yard, lying in the centre, was seen from every house in the parish. At length Burns arrived, mounted on a borrowed *pownie*. Instantly was the white flag hoisted, and as instantly were seen the farmers issuing from their houses, and converging to the point of meeting. A glorious evening, or rather night, which borrowed something from the morning, followed, and the conversation of the poet confirmed and increased the admiration created by his writings. On the following morning he breakfasted with a large party at the next farm-house, tenanted by James Stodart; ... took lunch with a large party at the bank in Carnwath, and rode into Edinburgh that evening on the *pownie*, which he returned to the owner in a few days afterwards by John Samson, the brother of the immortal *Tam*."

This is but a sample of the kind of receptions which were henceforth to await Burns wherever his coming was known. If such welcomes were pleasing to his ambition, they must have been trying both to his bodily and his mental health.

Burns reached Edinburgh on the 28th of November, 1786. The one man of note there with whom he had any acquaintance was Professor Dugald Stewart, whom, as already mentioned, he had met in Ayrshire. But it was not to him or to any one of his reputation that he first turned; but he sought refuge with John Richmond, an old Mauchline acquaintance, who was humbly lodged in Baxter's Close, Lawnmarket. During the whole of his first winter in Edinburgh, Burns lived in the lodging of this poor lad, and shared with him his single room and bed, for which they paid three shillings a week. It was from this retreat that Burns was afterwards to go forth into the best society of the Scottish capital, and thither, after these brief hospitalities were over, he had to return. For some days after his arrival in town, he called on no one—letters of introduction he had none to deliver. But he is said to have wandered about alone, "looking down from Arthur's Seat, surveying the palace, gazing at the Castle, or looking into the windows of the booksellers' shops, where he saw all books of the day, save the poems of the Ayrshire Ploughman." He found his way to the lowly grave of Fergusson, and, kneeling down, kissed the sod; he sought out the house of Allan Ramsay, and, on entering it, took off his hat. While Burns is thus employed, we may cast a glance at the capital to which he had come, and the society he was about to enter.

Edinburgh at that time was still adorned by a large number of the stars of literature, which, although none of those then living may have reached the first magnitude, had together made a galaxy in the northern heavens, from the middle till the close of last century. At that time literature was well represented in the University. The Head of it was Dr. Robertson, well known as the historian of Charles V., and as the author of other historic works. The chair of Belles-Lettres was filled by the accomplished Dr. Hugh Blair, whose lectures remain one of the best samples of the correct and elegant, but narrow and frigid style, both of sentiment and criticism, which then flourished throughout Europe, and nowhere more than in Edinburgh. Another still greater ornament of the University was Dugald Stewart, the Professor of Moral Philosophy, whose works, if they have often been surpassed in depth and originality of speculation, have seldom been equalled for solid sense and polished ease of diction. The professors at that time were most of them either taken from the ranks of the clergy, or closely connected with them.

Among the literary men unconnected with the University, by far the greatest name, that of David Hume, had disappeared about ten years before Burns arrived in the capital. But his friend, Dr. Adam Smith, author of *The Wealth of Nations*, still lingered. Mr. Henry Mackenzie,

"The Man of Feeling," as he was called from his best known work, was at that time one of the most polished as well as popular writers in Scotland. He was then conducting a periodical called the *Lounger*, which was acknowledged as the highest tribunal of criticism in Scotland, and was not unknown beyond it.

But even more influential than the literary lights of the University were the magnates of the Bench and Bar. During the eighteenth century and the earlier part of the nineteenth, the Scottish Bar was recruited almost entirely from the younger sons of ancient Scottish families. To the patrician feelings which they brought with them from their homes these men added that exclusiveness which clings to a profession claiming for itself the highest place in the city where they resided. Modern democracy has made rude inroads on what was formerly something of a select patrician caste. But the profession of the Bar has never wanted either then or in more recent times some genial and original spirits who broke through the crust of exclusiveness. Such, at the time of Burns's advent, was Lord Monboddo, the speculative and humorous judge, who in his own way anticipated the theory of man's descent from the monkey. Such, too, was the genial and graceful Henry Erskine, the brother of the Lord Chancellor of that name, the pride and the favourite of his profession—the sparkling and ready wit who, thirteen years before the day of Burns, had met the rude manners of Dr. Johnson with a well-known repartee. When the Doctor visited the Parliament House, Erskine was presented to him by Boswell, and was somewhat gruffly received. After having made his bow, Erskine slipped a shilling into Boswell's hand, whispering that it was for the sight of his *bear!*

Besides these two classes, the occupants of the Professorial chair and of the Bar, there still gathered every
winter in Edinburgh a fair sprinkling of rank and beauty,
which had not yet abandoned the Scottish for the English capital. The leader at that time in gay society was
the well-known Duchess of Gordon — a character so remarkable in her day that some rumour of her still lives
in Scottish memory. The impression made upon her by
Burns and his conversation shall afterwards be noticed.

Though Burns for the first day or two after his arrival
wandered about companionless, he was not left long unfriended. Mr. Dalrymple, of Orangefield, an Ayrshire
country gentleman, a warm - hearted man, and a zealous
Freemason, who had become acquainted with Burns during the previous summer, now introduced the Ayrshire
bard to his relative, the Earl of Glencairn. This nobleman, who had heard of Burns from his Ayrshire factor,
welcomed him in a very friendly spirit, introduced him to
his connexion, Henry Erskine, and also recommended him
to the good offices of Creech, at that time the first publisher in Edinburgh. Of Lord Glencairn, Chambers says
that "his personal beauty formed the index to one of the
fairest characters." As long as he lived he did his utmost to befriend Burns, and on his death, a few years after
this time, the poet, who seldom praised the great unless
he respected and loved them, composed one of his most
pathetic elegies.

It was not, however, to his few Ayrshire connexions
only, Mr. Dalrymple, Dugald Stewart, and others, that
Burns was indebted for his introduction to Edinburgh
society. His own fame was now enough to secure it. A
criticism of his poems, which appeared within a fortnight
after his arrival in Edinburgh, in the *Lounger*, on the

9th of December, did much to increase his reputation.
The author of that criticism was The Man of Feeling, and
to him belongs the credit of having been the first to claim
that Burns should be recognized as a great original poet,
not relatively only, in consideration of the difficulties he
had to struggle with, but absolutely on the ground of the
intrinsic excellence of his work.   He pointed to his power
of delineating manners, of painting the passions, and of
describing scenery, as all bearing the stamp of true genius;
he called on his countrymen to recognize that a great national poet had arisen amongst them, and to appreciate
the gift that in him had been bestowed upon their generation.   Alluding to his narrow escape from exile, he ex-
horted them to retain and to cherish this inestimable gift
of a native poet, and to repair, as far as possible, the
wrongs which suffering or neglect had inflicted on him.
The *Lounger* had at that time a wide circulation in Scotland, and penetrated even to England.   It was known and
read by the poet Cowper, who, whether from this or some
other source, became acquainted with the poems of Burns
within the first year of their publication.   In July, 1787,
we find the poet of *The Task* telling a correspondent that
he had read Burns's poems twice; "and though they be
written in a language that is new to me . . . I think
them, on the whole, a very extraordinary production.   He
is, I believe, the only poet these kingdoms have produced
in the lower rank of life since Shakespeare (I should rather
say since Prior), who need not be indebted for any part
of his praise to a charitable consideration of his origin,
and the disadvantages under which he has laboured."
Cowper thus endorses the verdict of Mackenzie in almost
the same language.

It did not, however, require such testimonials, from here

and there a literary man, however eminent, to open every
hospitable door in Edinburgh to Burns. Within a month
after his arrival in town he had been welcomed at the
tables of all the celebrities—Lord Monboddo, Robertson,
the historian, Dr. Hugh Blair, Dugald Stewart, Dr. Adam
Ferguson, The Man of Feeling, Mr. Fraser Tytler, and
many others. We are surprised to find that he had been
nearly two months in town before he called on the amiable
Dr. Blacklock, the blind poet, who in his well-known letter
to Dr. Laurie had been the first Edinburgh authority to
hail in Burns the rising of a new star.

How he bore himself throughout that winter when he
was the chief lion of Edinburgh society many records
remain to show, both in his own letters and in the reports
of those who met him. On the whole, his native good
sense carried him well through the ordeal. If he showed
for the most part due respect to others, he was still more
bent on maintaining his respect for himself; indeed, this
latter feeling was pushed even to an exaggerated independence. As Mr. Lockhart has expressed it, he showed,
"in the whole strain of his bearing, his belief that in the
society of the most eminent men of his nation he was
where he was entitled to be, hardly deigning to flatter
them by exhibiting a symptom of being flattered." All
who heard him were astonished by his wonderful powers
of conversation. These impressed them, they said, with a
greater sense of his genius than even his finest poems.

With the ablest men that he met he held his own in
argument, astonishing all listeners by the strength of his
judgment, and the keenness of his insight both into men
and things. And when he warmed on subjects which
interested him, the boldest stood amazed at the flashes of
his wit, and the vehement flow of his impassioned elo-

quence. With the "high-born ladies" he succeeded even better than with the "stately patricians"—as one of those dames herself expressed it, fairly carrying them off their feet by the deference of his manner, and the mingled humour and pathos of his talk.

It is interesting to know in what dress Burns generally appeared in Edinburgh. Soon after coming thither he is said to have laid aside his country clothes for "a suit of blue and buff, the livery of Mr. Fox, with buckskins and top-boots." How he wore his hair will be seen immediately. There are several well-known descriptions of Burns's manner and appearance during his Edinburgh sojourn, which, often as they have been quoted, cannot be passed by in any account of his life.

Mr. Walker, who met him for the first time at breakfast in the house of Dr. Blacklock, says, "I was not much struck by his first appearance. His person, though strong and well-knit, and much superior to what might be expected in a ploughman, appeared to be only of the middle size, but was rather above it. His motions were firm and decided, and, though without grace, were at the same time so free from clownish constraint as to show that he had not always been confined to the society of his profession. His countenance was not of that elegant cast which is most frequent among the upper ranks, but it was manly and intelligent, and marked by a thoughtful gravity which shaded at times into sternness. In his large dark eye the most striking index of his genius resided. It was full of mind. . . . He was plainly but properly dressed, in a style midway between the holiday costume of a farmer and that of the company with which he now associated. His black hair without powder, at a time when it was generally worn, was tied behind, and spread upon his fore-

3*

head.   Had I met him near a seaport, I should have con-
jectured him to be the master of a merchant vessel. . . .
In no part of his manner was there the slightest affectation ; nor could a stranger have suspected, from anything
in his behaviour or conversation, that he had been for some
months the favourite of all the fashionable circles of the
metropolis.   In conversation he was powerful.   His con-
ceptions and expressions were of corresponding vigour,
and on all subjects were as remote as possible from com-
monplaces.   Though somewhat authoritative, it was in a
way which gave little offence, and was readily imputed to
his inexperience in those modes of smoothing dissent and
softening assertion, which are important characteristics of
polished manners.

   " The day after my first introduction to Burns, I supped
with him at Dr. Blair's.   The other guests were few, and
as they had come to meet Burns, the Doctor endeavoured
to draw him out, and to make him the central figure of
the group.   Though he therefore furnished the greatest
proportion of the conversation, he did no more than what
he saw evidently was expected.   From the blunders often
committed by men of genius Burns was unusually free ;
yet on the present occasion he made a more awkward slip
than any that are reported of the poets or mathematicians
most noted for absence of mind.   Being asked from which
of the public places he had received the greatest gratification, he named the High Church, but gave the preference
as a preacher to the colleague of our worthy entertainer,
whose celebrity rested on his pulpit eloquence, in a tone so
pointed and decisive as to throw the whole company into
the most foolish embarrassment !"   Dr. Blair, we are told,
relieved their confusion by seconding Burns's praise.   The
poet saw his mistake, but had the good sense not to try to

7

repair it.   Years afterwards he told Professor Walker that
he had never spoken of this unfortunate blunder, so painful to him had the remembrance of it been.

There seems little doubt, from all the accounts that have
been preserved, that Burns in conversation gave forth his
opinions with more decision than politeness.   He had not
a little of that mistaken pride not uncommon among his
countrymen, which fancies that gentle manners and consideration for others' feelings are marks of servility.   He
was for ever harping on independence, and this betrayed
him into some acts of rudeness in society which have been
recorded with perhaps too great minuteness.

Against these remarks, we must set the testimony of
Dugald Stewart, who says: "The attentions he received
from all ranks and descriptions of persons would have turned any head but his own.   I cannot say that I perceived
any unfavourable effect which they left on his mind.   He
retained the same simplicity which had struck me so forcibly when first I saw him in the country, nor did he seem
to feel any additional self-importance from the number
and rank of his new acquaintance.   He walked with me
in spring, early in the morning, to the Braid Hills, when
he charmed me still more by his private conversation than
he had ever done in company.   He was passionately fond
of the beauties of nature; and he once told me, when I
was admiring a distant prospect in one of our morning
walks, that the sight of so many smoking cottages gave a
pleasure to his mind which none could understand who
had not witnessed, like himself, the happiness and worth
which they contained. . . . The idea which his conversation conveyed of the powers of his mind exceeded, if
possible, that which is suggested by his writings.   All his
faculties were, as far as I could judge, equally vigorous,

and his predilection for poetry was rather the result of his own enthusiastic and impassioned temper, than of a genius exclusively adapted to that species of composition. I should have pronounced him fitted to excel in whatever walk of ambition he had chosen. . . . The remarks he made on the characters of men were shrewd and pointed, though frequently inclining too much to sarcasm. His praise of those he loved was sometimes indiscriminate and extravagant. . . . His wit was ready, and always impressed with the marks of a vigorous understanding; but, to my taste, not often pleasing or happy."

While the learned of his own day were measuring him thus coolly, and forming their critical estimates of him, youths of the younger generation were regarding him with far other eyes. Of Jeffrey, when a lad in his teens, it is recorded that one day in the winter of 1786–87, as he stood on the High Street of Edinburgh, staring at a man whose appearance struck him, a person at a shop door tapped him on the shoulder and said, "Aye, laddie, ye may weel look at that man. That's Robbie Burns." This was the young critic's first and last look at the poet of his country.

But the most interesting of all the reminiscences of Burns, during his Edinburgh visit, or, indeed, during any other time, was the day when young Walter Scott met him, and received from him that one look of approbation.

This is the account of that meeting which Scott himself gave to Lockhart: "As for Burns, I may truly say, '*Virgilium vidi tantum.*' I was a lad of fifteen when he came to Edinburgh. I saw him one day at the late venerable Professor Adam Fergusson's. Of course we youngsters sat silent, looked and listened. The only thing I remembered which was remarkable in Burns's manner, was the effect produced upon him by a print of Bunbury's, representing a soldier lying dead on the snow, his dog sitting in misery on one side — on the other, his widow, with a child in her arms. These lines were written beneath:

> 'Cold on Canadian hills, or Minden's plain,
> Perhaps that parent wept her soldier slain—
> Bent o'er the babe, her eye dissolved in dew,
> The big drops mingling with the milk he drew,
> Gave the sad presage of his future years,
> The child of misery baptized in tears.'

"Burns seemed much affected by the print: he actually shed tears. He asked whose the lines were, and it chanced that nobody but myself remembered that they occur in a half-forgotten poem of Langhorne's, called by the unpromising title of The Justice of Peace. I whispered my information to a friend present, who mentioned it to Burns, who rewarded me with a look and a word, which though of mere civility, I then received with very great pleasure. His person was strong and robust; his manner rustic, not clownish; a sort of dignified plainness and simplicity. His countenance was more massive than it looks in any of the portraits. I would have taken the poet, had I not known who he was, for a very sagacious country farmer of the old Scotch school—the *douce gudeman* who held his own plough. There was a strong expression of sense and shrewdness in all his lineaments; the eye alone, I think, indicated the poetical character and temperament. It was large, and of a dark cast, which glowed (I say literally glowed) when he spoke with feeling or interest. I never saw such another eye in a human head, though I have seen the most distinguished men of my time."

While men of the upper ranks, old and young, were thus receiving their impressions, and forming their various estimates of Burns, he, we may be sure, was not behindhand in his reflections on them, and on himself. He had by nature his full share of that gnawing self-consciousness which haunts the irritable tribe, from which no modern poet but Walter Scott has been able wholly to escape. While he was bearing himself thus manfully to outward appearance, inwardly he was scrutinizing himself and others with a morbid sensitiveness. In the heyday of his Edinburgh popularity, he writes to Mrs. Dunlop, one of his most trusted friends, what he repeats to other correspondents, that he had long been at pains to take a true measure of himself and to form a just estimate of his powers; that this self-estimate was not raised by his present success, nor would it be depressed by future neglect; that though the tide of popularity was now at full flood, he foresaw that the ebb would soon set in, and that he was prepared for it. In the same letters he speaks of his having too much pride for servility, as though there was no third and more excellent way; of "the stubborn pride of his own bosom," on which he seems mainly to have relied. Indeed, throughout his life there is much talk of what Mr. Carlyle well calls the altogether barren and unfruitful principle of pride; much prating about "a certain fancied rock of independence"—a rock which he found but a poor shelter when the worst ills of life overtook him. This feeling reached its height when, soon after leaving Edinburgh, we find him writing to a comrade in the bitterness of his heart that the stateliness of Edinburgh patricians and the meanness of Mauchline plebeians had so disgusted him with his kind, that he had bought a pocket copy of Milton to study the character of Satan,

as the great exemplar of "intrepid, unyielding independence."

If during his stay in Edinburgh, his "irascible humour"
never went so far as this, "the contumely of condescension" must have entered pretty deeply into the soul of
the proud peasant when he made the following memorable
entry in his diary, on the 9th April, 1787. After some
remarks on the difficulty of true friendship, and the haz-
ard of losing men's respect by being too confidential with
friends, he goes on : "For these reasons, I am determined
to make these pages my confidant. I will sketch every
character that any way strikes me, to the best of my
power, with unshrinking justice. I will insert anecdotes
and take down remarks, in the old law phrase, without
feud or favour. . . . I think a lock and key a security at
least equal to the bosom of any friend whatever. My
own private story likewise, my love adventures, my ram-
bles; the frowns and smiles of fortune on my bardship;
my poems and fragments, that must never see the light,
shall be occasionally inserted. In short, never did four
shillings purchase so much friendship, since confidence
went first to the market, or honesty was set up for sale. . . .

"There are few of the sore evils under the sun give me
more uneasiness and chagrin, than the comparison how a
man of genius, nay, of avowed worth, is received everywhere, with the reception which a mere ordinary character, decorated with the trappings and futile distinctions of
fortune, meets : I imagine a man of abilities, his breast
glowing with honest pride, conscious that men are born
equal, still giving honour to whom honour is due; he
meets at a great man's table a Squire Something or a Sir
Somebody; he knows the noble landlord at heart gives
the bard, or whatever he is, a share of his good wishes, be-

yond, perhaps, any one at the table; yet how will it mortify him to see a fellow whose abilities would scarcely have made an eightpenny tailor, and whose heart is not worth three farthings, meet with attention and notice that are withheld from the son of genius and poverty!

"The noble Glencairn has wounded me to the soul here, because I dearly esteem, respect, and love him. He showed so much attention, engrossing attention, one day, to the only blockhead at table (the whole company consisted of his lordship, dunder-pate, and myself), that I was within half a point of throwing down my gage of contemptuous defiance, but he shook my hand and looked so benevolently good at parting, God bless him! though I should never see him more, I shall love him to my dying day! I am pleased to think I am so capable of gratitude, as I am miserably deficient in some other virtues."

Lockhart, after quoting largely from this Common-place Book, adds, "This curious document has not yet been printed entire. Another generation will, no doubt, see the whole of the confession." All that remains of it has recently been given to the world. The original design was not carried out, and what is left is but a fragment, written chiefly in Edinburgh, with a few additions made at Ellisland. The only characters which are sketched are those of Blair, Stewart, Creech, and Greenfield. The remarks on Blair, if not very appreciative, are mild and not unkindly. There seems to be irony in the praise of Dugald Stewart for the very qualities in which Burns probably thought him to be deficient. Creech's strangely composite character is well touched off. Dr. Greenfield, the colleague of Dr. Blair, whose eloquence Burns on an unfortunate occasion preferred to that of his host, alone comes in for an unaffected eulogy. The plain and manly directness of these prose sketches is in striking contrast to the ambitious flights which the poet attempts in many of his letters.

Dugald Stewart in his cautious way hints that Burns did not always keep himself to the learned circles which had welcomed him, but sometimes indulged in "not very select society." How much this cautious phrase covers may be seen by turning to Heron's account of some of the scenes in which Burns mingled. Tavern life was then in Edinburgh, as elsewhere, more or less habitual in all classes. In those clubs and brotherhoods of the middle class, which met in taverns down the closes and wynds of High Street, Burns found a welcome, warmer, freer, more congenial than any vouchsafed to him in more polished coteries. Thither convened when their day's work was done, lawyers, writers, schoolmasters, printers, shopkeepers, tradesmen—ranting, roaring boon-companions—who gave themselves up, for the time, to coarse songs, rough raillery, and deep drinking. At these meetings all restraint was cast to the winds, and the mirth drove fast and furious. With open arms the clubs welcomed the poet to their festivities; each man proud to think that he was carousing with Robbie Burns. The poet the while gave full vein to all his impulses, mimicking, it is said, and satirizing his superiors in position, who, he fancied, had looked on him coldly, paying them off by making them the butt of his raillery, letting loose all his varied powers, wit, humour, satire, drollery, and throwing off from time to time snatches of licentious song, to be picked up by eager listeners — song wildly defiant of all the proprieties. The scenes which Burns there took part in far exceeded any revelries he had seen in the clubs of

Tarbolton and Mauchline, and did him no good. If we
may trust the testimony of Heron, at the meetings of a
certain Crochallan club, and at other such uproarious gatherings, he made acquaintances who, before that winter was
over, led him on from tavern dissipations to still worse
haunts and habits.

By the 21st of April (1787), the ostensible object for
which Burns had come to Edinburgh was attained, and
the second edition of his poems appeared in a handsome
octavo volume. The publisher was Creech, then chief of
his trade in Scotland. The volume was published by subscription " for the sole benefit of the author," and the
subscribers were so numerous that the list of them covered thirty-eight pages. In that list appeared the names
of many of the chief men of Scotland, some of whom
subscribed for twenty — Lord Eglinton for as many as
forty-two copies. Chambers thinks that full justice has
never been done to the liberality of the Scottish public
in the way they subscribed for this volume. Nothing
equal to the patronage that Burns at this time met with
had been seen since the days of Pope's Iliad. This second edition, besides the poems which had appeared in the
Kilmarnock one, contained several additional pieces, the
most important of which had been composed before the
Edinburgh visit. Such were *Death and Doctor Hornbook*,
The Brigs of Ayr, *The Ordination*, *The Address to the
Unco Guid*. The proceeds from this volume ultimately
made Burns the possessor of about 500*l.*, quite a little
fortune for one who, as he himself confesses, had never
before had 10*l.* he could call his own. It would, however,
have been doubly welcome and useful to him, had it been
paid down without needless delay. But unfortunately

this was not Creech's way of transacting business, so that Burns was kept for many months waiting for a settlement — months during which he could not, for want of money, turn to any fixed employment, and which were therefore spent by him unprofitably enough.

CHAPTER III.

SOME small instalments of the profits of his new volume enabled our Poet, during the summer and autumn of 1787, to make several tours to various districts of Scotland, famous either for scenery or song. The day of regular touring had not yet set in, and few Scots at that time would have thought of visiting what Burns called the classic scenes of their country. A generation before this, poets in England had led the way in this—as when Gray visited the lakes of Cumberland, and Dr. Johnson the Highlands and the Western Isles. In his ardour to look upon places famous for their natural beauty or their historic associations, or even for their having been mentioned in some old Scottish song, Burns surpassed both Gray and Johnson, and anticipated the sentiment of the present century. Early in May he set out with one of his Crochallan club acquaintances, named Ainslie, on a journey to the Border. Ainslie was a native of the Merse, his father and family living in Dunse. Starting thence with Ainslie, Burns traversed the greater part of the vale of Tweed from Coldstream to Peebles, recalling, as he went along, snatches of song connected with the places he passed. He turned aside to see the valley of the Jed, and got as far as Selkirk in the hope of looking upon Yarrow. But from doing this he was hindered by a day of unceasing rain, and he who was so soon to become the chief singer of Scottish song was never allowed to look on that vale which has long been its most ideal home. Before finishing his tour, he went as far as Nithsdale, and surveyed the farm of Ellisland, with some thought already that he might yet become the tenant of it.

It is noteworthy, but not wonderful, that the scenes visited in this tour called forth no poetry from Burns, save here and there an allusion that occurred in some of his later songs. When we remember with what an uneasy heart Burns left Ayrshire for Edinburgh, that the town life he had there led for the last six months had done nothing to lighten—it had probably done something to increase the load of his mental disquietude—that in an illness which he had during his tour he confesses that "embittering remorse was scaring his fancy at the gloomy forebodings of death," and that when his tour was over, soon after his return to Edinburgh, he found the law let loose against him, and what was called a "fugæ" warrant issued for his apprehension, owing to some occurrence like to that which a year ago had terrified him with legal penalties, and all but driven him to Jamaica—when all these things are remembered, is it to be wondered that Burns should have wandered by the banks of Tweed, in no mood to chaunt beside it "a music sweeter than its own?"

At the close of his Border tour Burns had, as we have seen, visited Nithsdale and looked at the farm of Ellisland. From Nithsdale he made his way back to native Ayrshire and his family at Mossgiel. I have heard a tradition that his mother met him at the door of the small farm-house, with this only salutation, "O Robbie!" Neither Lockhart nor Chambers mentions this, but the latter says, his sister, Mrs. Begg, remembered the arrival of her brother. He

came in unheralded, and was in the midst of them before
they knew.   It was a quiet meeting, for the Mossgiel family had the true Scottish reticence or reserve; but though
their words were not "mony feck," their feelings were
strong.   It was, indeed, as strange a reverse as ever was
made by fortune's fickle wheel.   "He had left them," to
quote the words of Lockhart, "comparatively unknown,
his tenderest feelings torn and wounded by the behaviour
of the Armours, and so miserably poor that he had been
for some weeks obliged to skulk from the sheriff's officers
to avoid the payment of a paltry debt.   He returned, his
poetical fame established, the whole country ringing with
his praise, from a capital in which he was known to have
formed the wonder and delight of the polite and the learned; if not rich, yet with more money already than any of
his kindred had ever hoped to see him possess, and with
prospects of future patronage and permanent elevation in
the scale of society, which might have dazzled steadier eyes
than those of maternal and fraternal affection.   The proph-
et had at last honour in his own country, but the haughty
spirit that had preserved its balance in Edinburgh was not
likely to lose it at Mauchline."   The haughty spirit of
which Lockhart speaks was reserved for others than his
own family.   To them we hear of nothing but simple affection.   His youngest sister, Mrs. Begg, told Chambers,
"that her brother went to Glasgow, and thence sent home
a present to his mother and three sisters, namely, a quantity of *mode* silk, enough to make a bonnet and a cloak to
each, and a gown besides to his mother and youngest sister."   This was the way he took to mark their right to
share in his prosperity.   Mrs. Begg remembers going for
rather more than a week to Ayr to assist in making up
the dresses, and when she came back on a Saturday, her

brother had returned and requested her "to put on her dress that he might see how smart she looked in it." The thing that stirred his pride and scorn was the servility with which he was now received by his "plebeian brethren" in the neighbourhood, and chief among these by the Armours, who had formerly eyed him with looks askance. If any- thing "had been wanting to disgust me completely with Armour's family, their mean, servile compliance would have done it." So he writes, and it was this disgust that prompt- ed him to furnish himself, as we have seen he did, with a pocket copy of Milton, to study the character of Satan. This fierce indignation was towards the family; towards "bonny Jean" herself his feeling was far other. Having accidentally met her, his old affection revived, and they were soon as intimate as of old.

After a short time spent at Mossgiel wandering about, and once, it would seem, penetrating the West Highlands as far as Inverary, a journey during which his temper seems to have been far from serene, he returned in August to Edinburgh. There he encountered, and in time got rid of, the law troubles already alluded to; and on the 25th of August he set out, on a longer tour than any he had yet attempted, to the Northern Highlands.

The travelling companion whom he chose for this tour was a certain Mr. Nicol, whose acquaintance he seems to have first formed at the Crochallan club, or some other haunt of boisterous joviality. After many ups and downs in life Nicol had at last, by dint of some scholastic ability, settled as a master of the Edinburgh High School. What could have tempted Burns to select such a man for a fel- low-traveller? He was cast in one of nature's roughest moulds; a man of careless habits, coarse manners, enor- mous vanity, of most irascible and violent temper, which

vented itself in cruelties on the poor boys who were the
victims of his care.   Burns compared himself with such a
companion to "a man travelling with a loaded blunderbuss
at full cock."   Two things only are mentioned in his favour, that he had a warm heart, and an unbounded admiration of the poet.   But the choice of such a man was an
unfortunate one, and in the upshot did not a little to spoil
both the pleasure and the benefit which might have been
gathered from the tour.

Their journey lay by Stirling and Crieff to Taymouth
and Breadalbane, thence to Athole, on through Badenoch
and Strathspey to Inverness.   The return by the east coast
was through the counties of Moray and Banff to Aberdeen.
After visiting the county whence his father had come, and
his kindred who were still in Kincardineshire, Burns and
his companion passed by Perth back to Edinburgh, which
they reached on the 16th of September.   The journey oc-
cupied only two and twenty days, far too short a time to
see so much country, besides making several visits, with
any advantage.   During his Border tour Burns had ridden
his Rosinante mare, which he had named Jenny Geddes.
As his friend, the schoolmaster, was no equestrian, Burns
was obliged to make his northern journey in a post-chaise,
not the best way of taking in the varied and ever-chang-
ing sights and sounds of Highland scenery.

Such a tour as this, if Burns could have entered on it
under happier auspices, that is, with a heart at ease, a fitting companion, and leisure enough to view quietly the
scenes through which he passed, and to enjoy the society
of the people whom he met, could not have failed, from
its own interestingness, and its novelty to him, to have en-
riched his imagination, and to have called forth some lasting memorials.   As it was, it cannot be said to have done

either. There are, however, a few incidents which are worth noting. The first of these took place at Stirling. Burns and his companion had ascended the Castle Rock, to look on the blue mountain rampart that flanks the Highlands from Ben Lomond to Benvoirlich. As they were both strongly attached to the Stuart cause, they had seen with indignation, on the slope of the Castle hill, the ancient hall, in which the Scottish kings once held their Parliaments, lying ruinous and neglected. On returning to their inn, Burns, with a diamond he had bought for such purposes, wrote on the window-pane of his room some lines expressive of the disgust he had felt at that sight, concluding with some offensive remarks on the reigning family. The lines, which had no poetic merit, got into the newspapers of the day, and caused a good deal of comment. On a subsequent visit to Stirling, Burns himself broke the pane of the window on which the obnoxious lines were written, but they were remembered, it is said, long afterwards to his disadvantage.

Among the pleasantest incidents of the tour was the visit to Blair Castle, and his reception by the Duchess of Athole. The two days he spent there he declared were among the happiest of his life. We have seen how sensitive Burns was to the way he was received by the great. Resentful as he was equally of condescension and of neglect, it must have been no easy matter for persons of rank so to adapt their manner as to exactly please him. But his hosts at Blair Castle succeeded to admiration in this. They were assisted by the presence at the Castle of Mr., afterwards Professor, Walker, who had known Burns in Edinburgh, and was during that autumn living as a tutor in the Duke's family. At dinner Burns was in his most pleasing vein, and delighted his hostess by drinking to the

4

health of her group of fair young children, as "honest men
and bonny lassies"—an expression with which he happily
closes his *Petition of Bruar Water*. The Duchess had her
two sisters, Mrs. Graham and Miss Cathcart, staying with
her on a visit, and all three ladies were delighted with the
conversation of the poet. These three sisters were daugh-
ters of a Lord Cathcart, and were remarkable for their
beauty. The second, Mrs. Graham, has been immortalized
as the subject of one of Gainsborough's most famous portraits. On her early death her husband, Thomas Graham
of Balnagown, never again looked on that beautiful picture,
but left his home for a soldier's life, distinguished himself
greatly in the Peninsular War, and was afterwards known
as Lord Lynedoch. After his death, the picture passed
to his nearest relatives, who presented it to the National
Portrait Gallery of Scotland, of which it is now the chief
ornament. All three sisters soon passed away, having
died even before the short-lived poet. By their beauty
and their agreeableness they charmed Burns, and did much
to make his visit delightful. They themselves were not
less pleased; for when the poet proposed to leave, after
two days were over, they pressed him exceedingly to stay,
and even sent a messenger to the hotel to persuade the
driver of Burns's chaise to pull off one of the horse's shoes,
that his departure might be delayed. Burns himself would
willingly have listened to their entreaties, but his travelling
mate was inexorable. Likely enough Nicol had not been
made so much of as the poet, and this was enough to rouse
his irascible temper. For one day he had been persuaded
to stay by the offer of good trout-fishing, which he greatly relished, but now he insisted on being off. Burns was
reluctantly forced to yield.

This rapid departure was the more unfortunate because

Mr. Dundas, who held the keys of Scottish patronage, was expected on a visit to Blair, and had he met the poet he might have wiped out the reproach often cast on the ministry of the day, that they failed in their duty towards Burns. "That eminent statesman," as Lockhart says, "was, though little addicted to literature, a warm lover of his own country, and, in general, of whatever redounded to her honour; he was, moreover, very especially qualified to appreciate Burns as a companion; and had such an introduction taken place, he might not improbably have been induced to bestow that consideration on the claims of the poet, which, in the absence of any personal acquaintance, Burns's works ought to have received at his hands." But during that visit Burns met, and made the acquaintance of, another man of some influence, Mr. Graham of Fintray, whose friendship afterwards, both in the Excise business, and in other matters, stood him in good stead. The Duke, as he bade farewell to Burns at Blair, advised him to turn aside, and see the Falls of the Bruar, about six miles from the Castle, where that stream coming down from its mountains plunges over some high precipices, and passes through a rocky gorge to join the River Garry. Burns did so, and finding the falls entirely bare of wood, wrote some lines entitled *The Humble Petition of Bruar Water*, in which he makes the stream entreat the Duke to clothe its naked banks with trees. The poet's petition for the stream was not in vain. The then Duke of Athole was famous as a planter of trees, and those with which, after the poet's Petition, he surrounded the waterfall remain to this day.

After visiting Culloden Muir, the Fall of Fyers, Kilravock Castle, where, but for the impatience of Mr. Nicol, he would fain have prolonged his stay, he came on to Fochabers and Gordon Castle. This is Burns's entry in his diary:—" Cross Spey to Fochabers, fine palace, worthy of the noble, the polite, and generous proprietor. The Duke makes me happier than ever great man did; noble, princely, yet mild and condescending and affable—gay and kind. The Duchess, charming, witty, kind, and sensible. God bless them!"

Here, too, as at Blair, the ducal hosts seem to have entirely succeeded in making Burns feel at ease, and wish to protract his visit. But here, too, more emphatically than at Blair, his friend spoilt the game. This is the account of the incident, as given by Lockhart, with a few additions interpolated from Chambers :

" Burns, who had been much noticed by this noble family when in Edinburgh, happened to present himself at Gordon Castle just at the dinner-hour, and being invited to take a place at the table, did so, without for a moment adverting to the circumstance that his travelling companion had been left alone at the inn, in the adjacent village. On remembering this soon after dinner, he begged to be allowed to rejoin his friend; and the Duke of Gordon, who now for the first time learned that he was not journeying alone, immediately proposed to send an invitation to Mr. Nicol to come to the Castle. His Grace sent a messenger to bear it; but Burns insisted on himself accompanying him. They found the haughty schoolmaster striding up and down before the inn-door in a high state of wrath and indignation at, what he considered, Burns's neglect, and no apologies could soften his mood. He had already ordered horses, and was venting his anger on the postillion for the slowness with which he obeyed his commands. The poet, finding that he must choose between the ducal circle and his irascible associate, at once chose the latter alternative. Nicol and he, in silence and mutual displeasure, seated themselves in the post-chaise, and turned their backs on Gordon Castle, where the poet had promised himself some happy days. This incident may serve to suggest some of the annoyances to which persons moving, like our poet, on the debatable land between two different ranks of society must ever be subjected." "To play the lion under such circumstances must," as the knowing Lockhart observes, "be difficult at the best; but a delicate business indeed, when the jackals are presumptuous. The pedant could not stomach the superior success of his friend, and yet—alas for poor human nature!—he certainly was one of the most enthusiastic of his admirers, and one of the most affectionate of all his intimates." It seems that the Duchess of Gordon had some hope that her friend, Mr. Addington, afterwards Lord Sidmouth and the future premier, would have visited at Gordon Castle while Burns was there. Mr. Addington was, Allan Cunningham tells us, an enthusiastic admirer of Burns's poetry, and took pleasure in quoting it to Pitt and Melville. On that occasion he was unfortunately not able to accept the invitation of the Duchess, but he forwarded to her "these memorable lines—memorable as the first indication of that deep love which England now entertains for the genius of Burns:"

> "Yes! pride of Scotia's favoured plains, 'tis thine
> The warmest feelings of the heart to move;
> To bid it throb with sympathy divine,
> To glow with friendship, or to melt with love.

> "What though each morning sees thee rise to toil,
> Though Plenty on thy cot no blessing showers,
> Yet Independence cheers thee with her smile,
> And Fancy strews thy moorland with her flowers!

> " And dost thou blame the impartial will of Heaven,
>   Untaught of life the good and ill to scan ?
>   To thee the Muse's choicest wreath is given—
>   To thee the genuine dignity of man !

> " Then to the want of worldly gear resigned,
>   Be grateful for the wealth of thy exhaustless mind."

It was well enough for Mr. Addington, and such as he, to advise Burns to be content with the want of worldly gear, and to refer him for consolation to the dignity of man and the wealth of his exhaustless mind. Burns had abundance of such sentiments in himself to bring forth, when occasion required. He did not need to be replenished with these from the stores of men who held the keys of patronage. What he wanted from them was some solid benefit, such as they now and then bestowed on their favourites, but which unfortunately they withheld from Burns.

An intelligent boy, who was guide to Burns and Nicol from Cullen to Duff House, gave long afterwards his remembrances of that day. Among these this occurs. The boy was asked by Nicol if he had read Burns's poems, and which of them he liked best. The boy replied, " ' I was much entertained with *The Twa Dogs* and *Death and Dr. Hornbook*, but I like best *The Cotter's Saturday Night*, although it made me *greet* when my father had me to read it to my mother.' Burns, with a sudden start, looked at my face intently, and patting my shoulder, said, ' Well, my callant, I don't wonder at your *greeting* at reading the poem ; it made me greet more than once when I was writing it at my father's fireside.' " . . .

On the 16th of September, 1787, the two travellers returned to Edinburgh. This tour produced little poetry directly, and what it did produce was not of a high order.

In this respect one cannot but contrast it with the poetic results of another tour made, partly over the same ground, by another poet, less than twenty years after this time. When Wordsworth and his sister made their first visit to Scotland in 1803, it called forth some strains of such perfect beauty as will live while the English language lasts. Burns's poetic fame would hardly be diminished if all that he wrote on his tours were obliterated from his works. Perhaps we ought to except some allusions in his future songs, and especially that grand song, *Macpherson's Farewell*, which, though composed several months after this tour was over, must have drawn its materials from the day spent at Duff House, where he was shown the sword of the Highland Reiver.

But look at the lines composed after his first sight of Breadalbane, which he left in the inn at Kenmore. These Lockhart has pronounced among "the best of his purely English heroics" If so, we can but say how poor are the best! What is to be thought of such lines as

> " Poetic ardours in my bosom swell,
> Lone wandering by the hermit's mossy cell," etc., etc.

Nor less stilted, forced, and artificial are the lines in the same measure written at the Fall of Fyers.

The truth is, that Burns's *forte* by no means lay in describing scenery alone, and for its own sake. All his really inspired descriptions of it occur as adjuncts to human incident or feeling, slips of landscape let in as a background. Again, as Burns was never at his best when called on to write for occasions — no really spontaneous poet ever can be — so when taken to see much talked-of scenes, and expected to express poetic raptures over them, Burns did not answer to the call.

" He disliked," we are told, " to be tutored in matters
of taste, and could not endure that one should run shout-
ing before him, whenever any fine object came in sight."
On one occasion of this kind, a lady at the poet's side
said, " Burns, have you nothing to say of this ?"   " Nothing, madam," he replied, glancing at the leader of the
party, " for an ass is braying over it."   Burns is not the
only person who has suffered from this sort of officiousness.

Besides this, the tours were not made in the way which
most conduces to poetic composition.   He did not allow
himself the quiet and the leisure from interruption which
are needed.   It was not with such companions as Ainslie
or Nicol by his side that the poet's eye discovered new
beauty in the sight of a solitary reaper in a Highland glen,
and his ear caught magical suggestiveness in the words,
" What ! you are stepping westward," heard by the evening lake.

Another hindrance to happy poetic description by Burns
during these journeys was that he had now forsaken his
native vernacular, and taken to writing in English after
the mode of the poets of the day.   This with him was to
unclothe himself of his true strength.   His correspondent,
Dr. Moore, and his Edinburgh critics had no doubt coun-
selled him to write in English, and he listened for a time
too easily to their counsel.   He and they little knew what
they were doing in giving and taking such advice.   The
truth is, when he used his own Scottish dialect he was un-
approached, unapproachable ; no poet before or since has
evoked out of that instrument so perfect and so varied
melodies.   When he wrote in English he was seldom more
than third-rate ; in fact, he was but a common clever versi-
fier.   There is but one purely English poem of his which

at all approaches the first rank — the lines *To Mary in Heaven.*

These may probably have been the reasons, but the fact is certain that Burns's tours are disappointing in their direct poetic fruits. But in another way Burns turned them to good account. He had by that time begun to devote himself almost entirely to the cultivation of Scottish song. This was greatly encouraged by the appearance of *Johnson's Museum,* a publication in which an engraver of that name living in Edinburgh had undertaken to make a thorough collection of all the best of the old Scottish songs, accompanying them with the best airs, and to add to these any new songs of merit which he could lay hands on. Before Burns left Edinburgh for his Border tour, he had begun an acquaintance and correspondence with Johnson, and had supplied him with four songs of his own for the first volume of *The Museum.* The second volume was now in progress, and his labors for this publication, and for another of the same kind to be afterwards mentioned, henceforth engrossed Burns's entire productive faculty, and were to be his only serious literary work for the rest of his life. He therefore employed the Highland tour in hearing all he could, that had any bearing on his now absorbing pursuit, and in collecting materials that might promote it. With this view, when on his way from Taymouth to Blair, he had turned aside to visit the famous fiddler and composer of Scotch tunes, Neil Gow, at his house, which is still pointed out, at Inver, on the Braan Water, opposite the grounds of Dunkeld. This is the entry about him in Burns's diary : — " Neil Gow plays—a short, stout-built, honest Highland figure, with his grey hair shed on his honest social brow ; an interesting face marking strong sense, kind open-heartedness, mixed

4*

with unmistrusting simplicity; visit his house; Margaret Gow." It is interesting to think of this meeting of these two—the one a Lowlander, the other a Highlander; the one the greatest composer of words, the other of tunes, for Scottish songs, which their country has produced.

As he passed through Aberdeen, Burns met Bishop Skinner, a Bishop of the Scottish Episcopal Church; and when he learnt that the Bishop's father, the author of the song of *Tulloch-gorum*, and *The Ewie wi' the crookit horn*, and other Scottish songs, was still alive, an aged Episcopalian clergyman, living in primitive simplicity in *a but and a ben* at Lishart, near Peterhead, and that on his way to Aberdeen he had passed near the place without knowing it, Burns expressed the greatest regret at having missed seeing the author of songs he so greatly admired. Soon after his return to Edinburgh, he received from old Mr. Skinner a rhyming epistle, which greatly pleased the poet, and to which he replied—"I regret, and while I live shall regret, that when I was north I had not the pleasure of paying a younger brother's dutiful respect to the author of the best Scotch song ever Scotland saw, *Tulloch-gorum's my delight*." This is strong, perhaps too strong praise. Allan Cunningham, in his *Songs of Scotland*, thus freely comments on it :—" *Tulloch-gorum* is a lively clever song, but I would never have edited this collection had I thought with Burns that it is the best song Scotland ever saw. I may say with the king in my favourite ballad—

> "I trust I have within my realm,
> Five hundred good as he."

We also find Burns, on his return to Edinburgh, writing to the librarian at Gordon Castle to obtain from him a correct copy of a Scotch song composed by the Duke, in the current vernacular style, *Cauld Kail in Aberdeen*. This correct copy he wished to insert in the forthcoming volume of *Johnson's Museum*, with the name of the author appended.

At Perth he made inquiries, we are told, "as to the whereabouts of the burn-brae on which be the graves of Bessy Bell and Mary Gray." Whether he actually visited the spot, near the Almond Water, ten miles west of Perth, is left uncertain. The pathetic story of these two hapless maidens, and the fine old song founded on it, had made it to him a consecrated spot.

> "O Bessy Bell and Mary Gray!
>   They were twa bonny lasses,
> They biggit a bower on yon burn-brae,
>   And theekit it owre wi' rashes,"

is the beginning of a beautiful song which Allan Ramsay did his best to spoil, as he did in many another instance. Sir Walter Scott afterwards recovered some of the old verses which Ramsay's had superseded, and repeated them to Allan Cunningham, who gives them in his *Songs of Scotland*. Whether Burns knew any more of the song than the one old verse given above, with Ramsay's appended to it, is more than doubtful.

As he passed through Perth he secured an introduction to the family of Belches of Invermay, that, on crossing the River Earn on his southward journey, he might be enabled to see the little valley, running down from the Ochils to the Earn, which has been consecrated by the old and well-known song, *The Birks of Invermay*.

It thus appears that the old songs of Scotland, their localities, their authors, and the incidents whence they arose, were now uppermost in the thoughts of Burns, whatever part of his country he visited. This was as intense and as genuinely poetical an interest, though a more limited one, than that with which Walter Scott's eye afterwards ranged over the same scenes. The time was not yet full come for that wide and varied sympathy, with which Scott surveyed the whole past of his country's history, nor was Burns's nature or training such as to give him that catholicity of feeling which was required to sympathize, as Scott did, with all ranks and all ages. Neither could he have so seized on the redeeming virtues of rude and half-barbarous times, and invested them with that halo of romance which Scott has thrown over them. This romantic and chivalrous colouring was an element altogether alien to Burns's character. But it may well be, that these very limitations intensified the depth and vividness of sympathy with which Burns conceived the human situations portrayed in his best songs.

There was one more brief tour of ten days during October, 1787, which Burns made in the company of Dr. Adair. They passed first to Stirling, where Burns broke the obnoxious pane; then paid a second visit to Harvieston, near Dollar—for Burns had paid a flying visit of one day there, at the end of August, before passing northward to the Highlands—where Burns introduced his friend, and seems to have flirted with some Ayrshire young ladies, relations of his friend Gavin Hamilton. Thence they passed on a visit to Mr. Ramsay at Ochtertyre, on the Teith, a few miles west from Stirling. They then visited Sir William Murray at Ochtertyre, in Strathearn, where Burns wrote his *Lines on scaring some waterfowl in Lock Turit*, and a pretty pastoral song on a young beauty he met there, Miss Murray of Lintrose. From Strathearn he next seems to have returned by Clackmannan, there to visit the old lady

who lived in the Tower, of whom he had heard from Mr.
Ramsay. In this short journey the most memorable thing
was the visit to Mr. Ramsay at his picturesque old country
seat, situate on the River Teith, and commanding, down the
vista of its old lime-tree avenue, so romantic a view of
Stirling Castle rock. There Burns made the acquaintance
of Mr. Ramsay, the laird, and was charmed with the conversation of that "last of the Scottish line of Latinists,
which began with Buchanan and ended with Gregory"—
an antiquary, moreover, whose manners and home Lockhart thinks that Sir Walter may have had in his recollection when he drew the character of Monkbarns. Years
afterwards, in a letter addressed to Dr. Currie, Ramsay
thus wrote of Burns:—"I have been in the company of
many men of genius, some of them poets, but I never witnessed such flashes of intellectual brightness as from him,
the impulse of the moment, sparks of celestial fire. I
never was more delighted, therefore, than with his company two days *tête-à-tête*. In a mixed company I should
have made little of him; for, to use a gamester's phrase, he
did not know when to play off, and when to play on. . . .
When I asked whether the Edinburgh literati had mended
his poems by their criticisms, 'Sir,' said he, 'these gentlemen remind me of some spinsters in my country, who
spin their thread so fine, that it is neither fit for weft nor
woof.' "

There are other incidents recorded of that time.
Among these was a visit to Mrs. Bruce, an old Scottish
dame of ninety, who lived in the ancient Tower of Clackmannan, upholding her dignity as the lineal descendant
and representative of the family of King Robert Bruce,
and cherishing the strongest attachment to the exiled
Stuarts. Both of these sentiments found a ready response

from Burns. The one was exemplified by the old lady conferring knighthood on him and his companion with the actual sword of King Robert, which she had in her possession, remarking, as she did it, that she had a better right to confer the title than some folk. Another sentiment she charmed the poet by expressing in the toast she gave after dinner, "*Hooi Uncos*," that is, Away Strangers, a word used by shepherds when they bid their collies drive away strange sheep. Who the strangers were in this case may be guessed from her known Jacobite sentiments.

On his way from Clackmannan to Edinburgh he turned aside to see Loch Leven and its island castle, which had been the prison of the hapless Mary Stuart; and thence passing to the Norman Abbey Church of Dunfermline, with deep emotion he looked on the grave of Robert Bruce. At that time the choir of the old church, which had contained the grave, had been long demolished, and the new structure which now covers it had not yet been thought of. The sacred spot was only marked by two broad flagstones, on which Burns knelt and kissed them, reproaching the while the barbarity that had so dishonoured the resting-place of Scotland's hero king. Then, with that sudden change of mood so characteristic of him, he passed within the ancient church, and mounting the pulpit, addressed to his companion, who had, at his desire, mounted the cutty stool, or seat of repentance, a parody of the rebuke which he himself had undergone some time before at Mauchline.

CHAPTER IV.

THESE summer and autumn wanderings ended, Burns returned to Edinburgh, and spent there the next five months, from the latter part of October, 1787, till the end of March, 1788, in a way which to any man, much more to such an one as he, could give small satisfaction. The ostensible cause of his lingering in Edinburgh was to obtain a settlement with his procrastinating publisher, Creech, because, till this was effected, he had no money with which to enter on the contemplated farm, or on any other regular way of life. Probably in thus wasting his time, Burns may have been influenced more than he himself was aware, by a secret hope that something might yet be done for him—that all the smiles lavished on him by the great and powerful could not possibly mean nothing, and that he should be left to drudge on in poverty and obscurity as before.

During this winter Burns changed his quarters from Richmond's lodging in High Street, where he had lived during the former winter, to a house then marked 2, now 30, St. James's Square in the New Town. There he lived with a Mr. Cruikshank, a colleague of his friend Nicol in the High School, and there he continued to reside till he left Edinburgh. More than once he paid brief visits to Nithsdale, and examined again and yet again the farm on

the Dalswinton property, on which he had long had his
eye. This was his only piece of serious business during
those months. The rest of his time was spent more or
less in the society of his jovial companions. We hear no
more during this second winter of his meetings with literary professors, able advocates and judges, or fashionable
ladies. His associates seem to have been rather confined
to men of the Ainslie and Nicol stamp. He would seem
also to have amused himself with flirtations with several
young heroines, whose acquaintance he had made during
the previous summer. The chief of these were two young
ladies, Miss Margaret Chalmers and Miss Charlotte Hamilton, cousins of each other, and relatives of his Mauchline
friend, Gavin Hamilton. These he had met during the
two visits which he paid to Harvieston, on the River Devon, where they were living for a time. On his return to
Edinburgh he continued to correspond with them both,
and to address songs of affection, if not of love, now to
one, now to another. To Charlotte Hamilton he addressed
the song beginning—

> "How pleasant the banks of the clear winding Devon;"

To Miss Chalmers, one with the opening lines—

> "Where, braving angry winter's storms,
>   The lofty Ochils rise;"

And another beginning thus—

> "My Peggy's face, my Peggy's form."

Which of these young ladies was foremost in Burns's affection, it is not easy now to say, nor does it much signify.
To both he wrote some of his best letters, and some of not
his best verses. Allan Cunningham thinks that he had

serious affection for Miss Hamilton.   The latest editor of
his works asserts that his heart was set on Miss Chalmers,
and that she, long afterwards in her widowhood, told Thomas Campbell, the poet, that Burns had made a proposal of
marriage to her.   However this may be, it is certain that
while both admitted him to friendship, neither encouraged
his advances.   They were better " advised than to do so."
Probably they knew too much of his past history and his
character to think of him as a husband.   Both were soon
after this time married to men more likely to make them
happy than the erratic poet.   When they turned a deaf
ear to his addresses, he wrote : " My rhetoric seems to have
lost all its effect on the lovely half of mankind ; I have
seen the day—but that is a tale of other years.   In my conscience, I believe that my heart has been so often on fire
that it has been vitrified !"   Well perhaps for him if it
had been so, such small power had he to guide it.   Just
about the time when he found himself rejected, notwithstanding all his fine letters and his verses, by the two
young ladies on Devon banks, he met with an accident
through the upsetting of a hackney-coach by a drunken
driver.   The fall left him with a bruised limb, which confined him to his room from the 7th of December till the
middle of February (1788).

During these weeks he suffered much from low spirits,
and the letters which he then wrote under the influence of
that hypochondria and despondency contain some of the
gloomiest bursts of discontent with himself and with the
world, which he ever gave vent to either in prose or verse.
He describes himself as the " sport, the miserable victim
of rebellious pride, hypochondriac imagination, agonizing
sensibility, and Bedlam passions.   I wish I were dead, but
I'm no like to die. . . . I fear I am something like un-

done; but I hope for the best. Come, stubborn Pride and unshrinking Resolution; accompany me through this to me miserable world! I have a hundred times wished that one could resign life, as an officer resigns a commission; for I would not take in any poor wretch by selling out. Lately I was a sixpenny private, and, God knows, a miserable soldier enough; now I march to the campaign, a starving cadet—a little more conspicuously wretched."

But his late want of success on the banks of Devon, and his consequent despondency, were alike dispelled from his thoughts by a new excitement. Just at the time when he met with his accident, he had made the acquaintance of a certain Mrs. M'Lehose, and acquaintance all at once became a violent attachment on both sides. This lady had been deserted by her husband, who had gone to the West Indies, leaving her in poverty and obscurity to bring up two young boys as best she might. We are told that she was "of a somewhat voluptuous style of beauty, of lively and easy manners, of a poetical fabric of mind, with some wit, and not too high a degree of refinement or delicacy — exactly the kind of woman to fascinate Burns." Fascinated he certainly was. On the 30th December he writes: "Almighty love still reigns and revels in my bosom, and I am at this moment ready to hang myself for a young Edinburgh widow, who has wit and wisdom more murderously fatal than the assassinating stiletto of the Sicilian bandit, or the poisoned arrow of the savage African." For several months his visits to her house were frequent, his letters unremitting. The sentimental correspondence which they began, in which Burns addresses her as Clarinda, assuming to himself the name of Sylvander, has been published separately, and become notorious. Though this correspondence may contain, as Lockhart says, "passages of deep and noble feeling, which no one but Burns could have penned," it cannot be denied that it contains many more of such fustian, such extravagant bombast, as Burns or any man beyond twenty might well have been ashamed to write. One could wish that for the poet's sake this correspondence had never been preserved. It is so humiliating to read this torrent of falsetto sentiment now, and to think that a man gifted like Burns should have poured it forth. How far his feelings towards Clarinda were sincere, or how far they were wrought up to amuse his vacancy by playing at love-making, it is hard to say. Blended with a profusion of forced compliments and unreal raptures, there are expressions in Burns's letters which one cannot but believe that he meant in earnest, at the moment when he wrote them. Clarinda, it would seem, must have regarded Burns as a man wholly disengaged, and have looked forward to the possible removal of Mr. M'Lehose, and with him of the obstacle to a union with Burns. How far he may have really shared the same hopes it is impossible to say. We only know that he used again and again language of deepest devotion, vowing to "love Clarinda to death, through death, and for ever."

While this correspondence between Sylvander and Clarinda was in its highest flight of rapture, Burns received, in January or February, 1788, news from Mauchline which greatly agitated him. His renewed intercourse with Jean Armour had resulted in consequences which again stirred her father's indignation; this time so powerfully, that he turned his daughter to the door. Burns provided a shelter for her under the roof of a friend; but for a time he does not seem to have thought of doing more than this. Whether he regarded the original private marriage as entirely dissolved, and looked on himself as an unmarried

man, does not quite appear. Anyhow, he and Clarinda,
who knew all that had passed with regard to Jean Armour,
seem to have then thought that enough had been done
for the seemingly discarded Mauchline damsel, and to have
carried on their correspondence as rapturously as ever for
fully another six weeks, until the 21st of March (1788).
On that day Sylvander wrote to Clarinda a final letter,
pledging himself to everlasting love, and following it by a
copy of verses beginning—

           "Fair empress of the poet's soul,"

presenting her at the same time with a pair of wine-glasses
as a parting gift.

   On the 24th of March, he turned his back on Edinburgh,
and never returned to it for more than a day's visit.

   Before leaving town, however, he had arranged three
pieces of business, all bearing closely on his future life.
First, he had secured for himself an appointment in the
Excise through the kindness of " Lang Sandy Wood," the
surgeon who attended him when laid up with a bruised
limb, and who had interceded with Mr. Graham of Fintray,
the chief of the Excise Board, on Burns's behalf. When
he received his appointment, he wrote to Miss Chalmers,
"I have chosen this, my dear friend, after mature delibera-
tion. The question is not at what door of fortune's palace
shall we enter in, but what doors does she open for us. I
was not likely to get anything to do. I got this without
hanging-on, or mortifying solicitation ; it is immediate
bread, and though poor in comparison of the last eighteen
months of my existence, 'tis luxury in comparison of all
my preceding life."

   Next, he had concluded a bargain with Mr. Miller of
Dalswinton, to lease his farm of Ellisland, on which he

had long set his heart, and to which he had paid several visits in order to inspect it.

Lastly, he had at last obtained a business settlement with Creech regarding the Second Edition of his Poems. Before this was effected, Burns had more than once lost his temper, and let Creech know his mind. Various accounts have been given of the profits that now accrued to Burns from the whole transaction. We cannot be far wrong in taking the estimate at which Dr. Chambers arrived, for on such a matter he could speak with authority. He sets down the poet's profits at as nearly as possible 500*l.* Of this sum Burns gave 180*l.* to his brother Gilbert, who was now in pecuniary trouble. "I give myself no airs on this," he writes, "for it was mere selfishness on my part; I was conscious that the wrong scale of the balance was pretty heavily charged, and I thought that throwing a little filial piety and fraternal affection into the scale in my favour, might help to smooth matters at the grand reckoning." This money was understood by the family to be the provision due from Robert on behalf of his mother, the support of whom he was, now that he was setting up for himself, about to throw on his younger brother. Chambers seems to reckon that as another 120*l.* must have been spent by Burns on his tours, his accident, and his sojourn in Edinburgh since October, he could not have more than 200*l.* over, with which to set up at Ellisland. We see in what terms Burns had written to Clarinda on the 21st of March. On his leaving Edinburgh and returning to Ayrshire, he married Jean Armour, and forthwith acknowledged her in letters as his wife. This was in April, though it was not till August that he and Jean appeared before the Kirk-Session, and were formally recognized as man and wife by the Church.

Whether, in taking this step, Burns thought that he was carrying out a legal, as well as a moral, obligation, we know not. The interpreters of the law now assert that the original marriage in 1786 had never been dissolved, and that the destruction of the promissory lines, and the temporary disownment of him by Jean and her family, could not in any way invalidate it. Indeed, after all that had happened, for Burns to have deserted Jean, and married another, even if he legally could have done so, would have been the basest infidelity. Amid all his other errors and inconsistencies—and no doubt there were enough of these—we cannot but be glad for the sake of his good name that he now acted the part of an honest man, and did what he could to repair the much suffering and shame he had brought on his frail but faithful Jean.

As to the reasons which determined Burns to marry Jean Armour, and not another, this is the account he himself gives when writing to Mrs. Dunlop, one of his most trusted correspondents, to whom he spoke out his real heart in a simpler, more natural way, than was usual with him in letter-writing:

"You are right that a bachelor state would have ensured me more friends; but, from a cause you will easily guess, conscious peace in the enjoyment of my own mind, and unmistrusting confidence in approaching my God, would seldom have been of the number. I found a once much-loved, and still much-loved, female, literally and truly cast out to the mercy of the naked elements; but I enabled her to purchase a shelter;—there is no sporting with a fellow-creature's happiness or misery. The most placid good-nature and sweetness of disposition; a warm heart, gratefully devoted with all its powers to love me; vigorous health and sprightly cheerfulness, set off to the best ad-

vantage by a more than commonly handsome figure : these,
I think, in a woman may make a good wife, though she
should never have read a page but the Scriptures of the
Old and New Testament, nor have danced in a brighter
assembly than a penny pay wedding."

To Miss Chalmers he says:

" I have married my Jean. I had a long and much-
loved fellow-creature's happiness or misery in my determi-
nation, and I durst not trifle with so important a deposit,
nor have I any cause to repent it. If I have not got polite
tittle-tattle, modish manners, and fashionable dress, I am not
sickened and disquieted with the multiform curse of board-
ing-school affectation ; and I have got the handsomest figure, the sweetest temper, the soundest constitution, and the
kindest heart in the country. . . . A certain late publication of Scots poems she has perused very devoutly, and all
the ballads in the country, as she has the finest wood-note
wild I ever heard."

There have been many comments on this turning-point
in Burns's life. Some have given him high praise for it,
as though he had done a heroic thing in voluntarily sac-
rificing himself, when it might have been open to him to
form a much higher connexion. But all such praise seems
entirely thrown away. It was not, as it appears, open to
him to form any other marriage legally ; certainly it was
not open to him morally. The remark of Lockhart is entirely true, that, " had he hesitated to make her his wife,
whom he loved, and who was the mother of his children,
he must have sunk into the callousness of a ruffian."
Lockhart need hardly have added, " or into that misery of
miseries, the remorse of a poet."

But even had law and morality allowed him to pass by
Jean—which they did not—would it have been well for

Burns, if he had sought, as one of his biographers regrets
that he had not done, a wife among ladies of higher rank
and more refined manners? That he could appreciate what
these things imply, is evident from his own confession in
looking back on his introduction to what is called society: "A refined and accomplished woman was a being altogether new to me, and of which I had formed a very inade-
quate idea." It requires but little knowledge of the world
and its ways to see the folly of all such regrets. Great
disparity of condition in marriage seldom answers. And
in the case of a wayward, moody man, with the pride, the
poverty, and the irregularities of Burns, and the drudging
toil which must needs await his wife, it is easy to see what
misery such a marriage would have stored up for both.
As it was, the marriage he made was, to put it at the lowest, one of the most prudent acts of his life. Jean proved
to be all, and indeed more than all, he anticipates in the
letters above given. During the eight years of their married life, according to all testimony, she did her part as a
wife and mother with the most patient and placid fidelity,
and bore the trials which her husband's irregular habits entailed on her, with the utmost long-suffering. And after
his death, during her long widowhood, she revered his
memory, and did her utmost to maintain the honour of
his name.

With his marriage to his Ayrshire wife, Burns had bid
farewell to Edinburgh, and to whatever high hopes it may
have at any time kindled within him, and had returned to
a condition somewhat nearer to that in which he was born.
With what feelings did he pass from this brilliant interlude, and turn the corner which led him back to the dreary
road of commonplace drudgery, which he hoped to have
escaped? There can be little doubt that his feelings were

those of bitter disappointment. There had been, it is said, a marked contrast between the reception he had met with during his first and second winters in Edinburgh. As Allan Cunningham says, " On his first appearance the doors of the nobility opened spontaneously, ' on golden hinges turning,' and he ate spiced meats and drank rare wines, interchanging nods and smiles with high dukes and mighty earls. A colder reception awaited his second coming. The doors of lords and ladies opened with a tardy courtesy; he was received with a cold and measured stateliness, was seldom requested to stop, seldomer to repeat his visit; and one of his companions used to relate with what indignant feeling the poet recounted his fruitless calls and his uncordial receptions in the good town of Edinburgh. . . . He went to Edinburgh strong in the belief that genius such as his would raise him in society; he returned not without a sourness of spirit and a bitterness of feeling."

When he did give vent to his bitterness, it was not into man's, but into woman's sympathetic ear that he poured his complaint. It is thus he writes, some time after settling at Ellisland, to Mrs. Dunlop, showing how fresh was still the wound within. " When I skulk into a corner lest the rattling equipage of some gaping blockhead should mangle me in the mire, I am tempted to exclaim, ' What merits has he had, or what demerit have I had, in some previous state of existence, that he is ushered into this state of being with the sceptre of rule, and the keys of riches in his puny fist, and I am kicked into the world, the sport of folly, or the victim of pride? . . . Often as I have glided with humble stealth through the pomp of Princes Street, it has suggested itself to me, as an improvement on the present human figure, that a man, in

5

proportion to his own conceit of his own consequence in
the world, could have pushed out the longitude of his
common size, as a snail pushes out his horns, or as we
draw out a prospect-glass.' "

This is a feeling which Burns has uttered in many a
form of prose and verse, but which probably never possessed him more bitterly than when he retired from Edinburgh. Many persons in such circumstances may have felt
thoughts of this kind pass over them for a moment. But
they have felt ashamed of them as they rose, and have at
once put them by. Burns no doubt had a severer trial in
this way than most, but he never could overcome it, never
ceased to chafe at that inequality of conditions which is
so strongly fixed in the system in which we find ourselves.

It was natural that he should have felt some bitterness
at the changed countenance which Edinburgh society
turned on him, and it is easy to be sarcastic on the upper
ranks of that day for turning it: but were they really so
much to blame? There are many cases under the present
order of things, in which we are constrained to say, "It
must needs be that offences come." Taking men and
things as they are, could it well have been otherwise?

First, the novelty of Burns's advent had worn off by his
second winter in Edinburgh, and, though it may be a
weakness, novelty always counts for something in human
affairs. Then, again, the quiet, decorous men of Blair's
circle knew more of Burns's ways and doings than at first,
and what they came to know was not likely to increase
their desire for intimacy with him. It was, it seems, notorious that Burns kept that formidable memorandum-
book already alluded to, in which he was supposed to
sketch with unsparing hand, "stern likenesses" of his
friends and benefactors. So little of a secret did he make

of this, that we are told he sometimes allowed a visitor to have a look at the figures which he had sketched in his portrait-gallery. The knowledge that such a book existed was not likely to make Blair and his friends more desirous of his society.

Again, the festivities at the Crochallan Club and other such haunts, the habits he there indulged in, and the associates with whom he consorted, these were well known. And it was not possible that either the ways, the conversation, or the cronies of the Crochallan Club could be welcomed in quieter and more polished circles. Men of the Ainslie and Nicol stamp would hardly have been quite in place there.

Again—what is much to the honour of Burns—he never, in the highest access of his fame, abated a jot of his intimacy and friendship towards the men of his own rank, with whom he had been associated in his days of obscurity. These were tradesmen, farmers, and peasants. The thought of them, their sentiments, their prejudices and habits, if it had been possible, their very persons, he would have taken with him, without disguise or apology, into the highest circles of rank or of literature. But this might not be. It was impossible that Burns could take Mauchline with its belles, its Poosie-Nansies and its Souter Johnnies, bodily into the library of Dr. Blair or the drawing-room of Gordon Castle.

A man, to whom it is open, must make his choice; but he cannot live at once in two different and widely sundered orders of society. To no one is it given, not even to men of genius great as that of Burns, for himself and his family entirely to overleap the barriers with which custom and the world have hedged us in, and to weld the extremes of

society into one. To the speculative as well as to the practically humane man, the great inequality in human conditions presents, no doubt, a perplexing problem. A little less worldly pride, and a little more Christian wisdom and humility, would probably have helped Burns to solve it better than he did. But besides the social grievance, which though impalpable is very real, Burns had another more material and tangible. The great whom he had met in Edinburgh, whose castles he had visited in the country, might have done something to raise him at once above poverty and toil, and they did little or nothing. They had, indeed, subscribed liberally for his Second Edition, and they had got him a gauger's post, with fifty or sixty pounds a year—that was all. What more could they, ought they to have done? To have obtained him an office in some one of the higher professions was not to be thought of, for a man cannot easily, at the age of eight-and-twenty, change his whole line and adapt himself to an entirely new employment. The one thing they might have combined to do, was to have compelled Dundas, or some other of the men then in power, to grant Burns a pension from the public purse. That was the day of pensions, and hundreds with no claim to compare with Burns's were then on the pension list: 300*l.* a year would have sufficed to place him in comfort and independence; and could public money have been better spent? But though the most rigid economist might not have objected, would Burns have accepted such a benefaction, had it been offered? And if he had accepted it, would he not have chafed under the obligation, more even than he did in the absence of it? Such questions as these cannot but arise, as often as we think over the fate of Burns, and ask ourselves if nothing could have been done to avert it. Though natural, they are vain. Things hold on their own course to their inevitable issues, and Burns left Edinburgh, and set his face first towards Ayrshire, then to Nithsdale, a saddened and embittered man.

CHAPTER V.

"MR. BURNS, you have made a poet's not a farmer's choice." Such was the remark of Allan Cunningham's father, land-steward to the laird of Dalswinton, when the poet turned from the low-lying and fertile farm of Foregirth, which Cunningham had recommended to him, and selected for his future home the farm of Ellisland. He was taken by the beautiful situation and fine romantic outlook of the poorest of several farms on the Dalswinton estate which were in his option. Ellisland lies on the western bank of the River Nith, about six miles above Dumfries. Looking from Ellisland eastward across the river, "a pure stream running there over the purest gravel," you see the rich holms and noble woods of Dalswinton. Dalswinton is an ancient historic place, which has even within recorded memory more than once changed its mansion-house and its proprietor. To the west the eye falls on the hills of Dunscore, and looking northward up the Nith, the view is bounded by the heights that shut in the river towards Drumlanrig, and by the high conical hill of Corsincon, at the base of which the infant stream slips from the shire of Ayr into that of Dumfries. The farmsteading of Ellisland stands but a few yards to the west of the Nith. Immediately underneath there is a red scaur of considerable height, overhanging the stream, and the rest of the bank is covered with broom, through which winds a greensward path, whither Burns used to retire to meditate his songs. The farm extends to upwards of a hundred acres, part holm, part croft-land, of which the former yielded good wheat, the latter oats and potatoes. The lease was for nineteen years, and the rent fifty pounds for the first three years; seventy for the rest of the tack. The laird of Dalswinton, while Burns leased Ellisland, was Mr. Patrick Millar, not an ordinary laird, but one well known in his day for his scientific discoveries. There was no proper farm-house or offices on the farm—it was part of the bargain that Burns should build these for himself. The want of a house made it impossible for him to settle at once on his farm. His bargain for it had been concluded early in March (1788); but it was not till the 13th of June that he went to reside at Ellisland. In the interval between these two dates he went to Ayrshire, and completed privately, as we have seen, the marriage, the long postponement of which had caused him so much disquiet. With however great disappointment and chagrin he may have left Edinburgh, the sense that he had now done the thing that was right, and had the prospect of a settled life before him, gave him for a time a peace and even gladness of heart, to which he had for long been a stranger. We can, therefore, well believe what he tells us, that, when he had left Edinburgh, he journeyed towards Mauchline with as much gaiety of heart " as a May-frog, leaping across the newly-harrowed ridge, enjoying the fragrance of the refreshed earth after the long-expected shower." Of what may be called the poet's marriage settlement, we have the following details from Allan Cunningham:

" His marriage reconciled the poet to his wife's kindred: there was no wedding portion. Armour was a respectable man, but not opulent. He gave his daughter some small store of plenishing; and, exerting his skill as a mason, wrought his already eminent son-in-law a handsome punch-bowl in Inverary marble, which Burns lived to fill often, to the great pleasure both of himself and his friends. . . . Mrs. Dunlop bethought herself of Ellisland, and gave a beautiful heifer; another friend contributed a plough. The young couple, from love to their native county, ordered their furniture from a wright in Mauchline; the farm-servants, male and female, were hired in Ayrshire, a matter of questionable prudence, for the mode of cultivation is different from that of the west, and the cold, humid bottom of Mossgiel bears no resemblance to the warm and stony loam of Ellisland."

When on the 13th June he went to live on his farm, he had, as there was no proper dwelling-house on it, to leave Jean and her one surviving child behind him at Mauchline, and himself to seek shelter in a mere hovel on the skirts of the farm. "I remember the house well," says Cunningham, "the floor of clay, the rafters japanned with soot, the smoke from a hearth-fire streamed thickly out at door and window, while the sunshine which struggled in at those apertures produced a sort of twilight." Burns thus writes to Mrs. Dunlop, "A solitary inmate of an old smoky spence, far from every object I love or by whom I am beloved; nor any acquaintance older than yesterday, except Jenny Geddes, the old mare I ride on, while uncouth cares and novel plans hourly insult my awkward ignorance and bashful inexperience." It takes a more even, better-ordered spirit than Burns's to stand such solitude. His heart, during those first weeks at Ellisland, entirely sank within him, and he saw all men and life coloured by his own despondency. This is the entry in his commonplace book on the first Sunday he spent alone at Ellisland:—"I am such a coward in life, so tired of the service, that I would almost at any time, with Milton's Adam, 'gladly lay me in my mother's lap, and be at peace.' But a wife and children bind me to struggle with the stream, till some sudden squall shall overset the silly vessel, or in the listless return of years its own craziness reduce it to wreck."

The discomfort of his dwelling-place made him not only discontented with his lot, but also with the people amongst whom he found himself. "I am here," he writes, "on my farm; but for all the pleasurable part of life called social communication, I am at the very elbow of existence. The only things to be found in perfection in this country are stupidity and canting. . . . As for the Muses, they have as much idea of a rhinoceros as a poet."

When he was not in Ayrshire in bodily presence, he was there in spirit. It was at such a time that, looking up to the hills that divide Nithsdale from Ayrshire, he breathed to his wife that most natural and beautiful of all his love-lyrics—

> "Of a' the airts the wind can blaw
> I dearly like the west,
> For there the bonnie lassie lives,
> The lassie I lo'e best."

His disparagement of Nithsdale people, Allan Cunningham, himself a Dumfriesshire man, naturally resents, and accounts for it by supposing that the sooty hovel had infected his whole mental atmosphere. "The Maxwells, the Kirkpatricks, and Dalzells," exclaims honest Allan, "were fit companions for any man in Scotland, and they were almost his neighbours; Riddell of Friars Carse, an accomplished antiquarian, lived almost next door; and Jean

5*

Lindsay and her husband, Patrick Millar, the laird of
Dalswinton, were no ordinary people. The former, beautiful, accomplished, a writer of easy and graceful verses,
with a natural dignity of manners which became her
station; the latter an improver and inventor, the first who
applied steam to the purposes of navigation." But Burns's
hasty judgments of men and things, the result of momentary feeling, are not to be too literally construed.

He soon found that there was enough of sociality
among all ranks of Dumfriesshire people, from the laird
to the cotter, indeed, more than was good for himself.
Yet, however much he may have complained, when writing letters to his correspondents of an evening, he was too
manly to go moping about all day long when there was
work to be done. He was, moreover, nerved to the task
by the thought that he was preparing the home that was
to shelter his wife and children. On the laying of the
foundation-stone of his future house, he took off his hat
and asked a blessing on it. "Did he ever put his own
hand to the work?" was asked of one of the men engaged
in it. "Ay, that he did, mony a time," was the answer;
"if he saw us like to be beat wi' a big stane, he would
cry, 'Bide a wee,' and come rinning. We soon found out
when he put to his hand, he beat a' I ever met for a dour
lift."

During his first harvest, though the weather was unfavourable, and the crop a poor one, we find Burns speaking in his letters of being industriously employed, and
binding every day after the reapers. But Allan Cunningham's father, who had every opportunity of observing,
used to allege that Burns seemed to him like a restless
and unsettled man. "He was ever on the move, on foot
or on horseback. In the course of a single day he might

be seen holding the plough, angling in the river, saun-
tering, with his hands behind his back, on the banks,
looking at the running water, of which he was very fond,
walking round his buildings or over his fields ; and if you
lost sight of him for an hour, perhaps you might see him
returning from Friars Carse, or spurring his horse through
the hills to spend an evening in some distant place with
such friends as chance threw in his way." Before his
new house was ready, he had many a long ride to and
fro through the Cumnock hills to Mauchline, to visit Jean,
and to return. It was not till the first week of December, 1788, that his lonely bachelor life came to an end,
and that he was able to bring his wife and household to
Nithsdale. Even then the house at Ellisland was not
ready for his reception, and he and his family had to put
up for a time in a neighbouring farm-house called the Isle.
They brought with them two farm-lads from Ayrshire,
and a servant lass called Elizabeth Smith, who was alive
in 1851, and gave Chambers many details of the poet's
way of life at Ellisland. Among these she told him that
her father was so concerned about her moral welfare that,
before allowing her to go, he made Burns promise to keep
a strict watch over her behaviour, and to exercise her duly
in the Shorter Catechism ; and that both of these promises
he faithfully fulfilled.

The advent of his wife and his child in the dark days
of the year kept dulness aloof, and made him meet the
coming of the new year (1789) with more cheerful hopes
and calmer spirits than he had known for long. Alas,
that these were doomed to be so short-lived !

On New-Year's morning, 1789, his brother Gilbert thus
affectionately writes to the poet : " Dear Brother,—I have
just finished my New-Year's Day breakfast in the usual

form, which naturally makes me call to mind the days of former years, and the society in which we used to begin them; and when I look at our family vicissitudes, 'through the dark postern of time long elapsed,' I cannot help remarking to you, my dear brother, how good the God of seasons is to us, and that, however some clouds may seem to lower over the portion of time before us, we have great reason to hope that all will turn out well." On the same New-Year's Day Burns addressed to Mrs. Dunlop a letter, which, though it has been often quoted, is too pleasing to be omitted here. " I own myself so little a Presbyterian, that I approve set times and seasons of more than ordinary acts of devotion for breaking in on that habituated routine of life and thought, which is so apt to reduce our existence to a kind of instinct, or even sometimes, and with some minds, to a state very little superior to mere machinery. This day—the first Sunday of May—a breezy, blue-skied noon some time about the beginning, and a hoary morning and calm sunny day about the end, of autumn—these, time out of mind, have been with me a kind of holiday. . . . We know nothing, or next to nothing, of the substance or structure of our souls, so cannot account for those seeming caprices in them, that we should be particularly pleased with this thing, or struck with that, which on minds of a different cast makes no extraordinary impression. I have some favourite flowers in spring, among which are the mountain-daisy, the harebell, the fox-glove, the wild-brier rose, the budding birch, and the hoary hawthorn, that I view and hang over with particular delight. I never hear the loud, solitary whistle of the curlew in a summer noon, or the wild, mixing cadence of a troop of gray plovers in an autumnal morning, without feeling an elevation of soul like the enthusiasm of devotion or poetry. Tell me, my

dear friend, to what can this be owing? Are we a piece
of machinery, which, like the Æolian harp, passive, takes
the impression of the passing accident? Or do these
workings argue something within us above the trodden
clod? I own myself partial to such proofs of those awful
and important realities — a God that made all things —
man's immaterial and immortal nature—and a world of
weal or woe beyond death and the grave!"

On reading this beautiful and suggestive letter, an orni-
thologist remarked that Burns had made a mistake in a
fact of natural history. It is not the 'gray plover,' but
the golden, whose music is heard on the moors in autumn.
The gray plover, our accurate observer remarks, is a winter shore bird, found only at that season and in that hab-
itat, in this country.

It was not till about the middle of 1789 that the farm-
house of Ellisland was finished, and that he and his family,
leaving the Isle, went to live in it. When all was ready,
Burns bade his servant, Betty Smith, take a bowl of salt,
and place the Family Bible on the top of it, and, bearing
these, walk first into the new house and possess it. He
himself, with his wife on his arm, followed Betty and the
Bible and the salt, and so they entered their new abode.
Burns delighted to keep up old-world *freits* or usages like
this. It was either on this occasion, or on his bringing
Mrs. Burns to the Isle, that he held a house-heating mentioned by Allan Cunningham, to which all the neighbourhood gathered, and drank, " Luck to the roof-tree of the
house of Burns!" The farmers and the well-to-do people welcomed him gladly, and were proud that such a
man had come to be a dweller in their vale. Yet the
ruder country lads and the lower peasantry, we are told,
looked on him not without dread, " lest he should pickle

and preserve them in sarcastic song." "Once at a penny
wedding, when one or two wild young lads quarrelled, and
were about to fight, Burns rose up and said, 'Sit down
and ——, or else I'll hang you up like potato-bogles in
sang to-morrow.' They ceased, and sat down as if their
noses had been bleeding."

The house which had cost Burns so much toil in build-
ing, and which he did not enter till about the middle of
the year 1789, was a humble enough abode. Only a large
kitchen, in which the whole family, master and servants,
took their meals together, a room to hold two beds, a
closet to hold one, and a garret, coom-ceiled, for the female servants, this made the whole dwelling-house. "One
of the windows looked southward down the holms; another opened on the river; and the house stood so near
the lofty bank, that its afternoon shadow fell across the
stream, on the opposite fields. The garden or kail-yard
was a little way from the house. A pretty footpath led
southward along the river side, another ran northward, af-
fording fine views of the Nith, the woods of Friars Carse,
and the grounds of Dalswinton. Half-way down the
steep declivity, a fine clear cool spring supplied water to
the household." Such was the first home which Burns
found for himself and his wife, and the best they were
ever destined to find. The months spent in the Isle, and
the few that followed the settlement at Ellisland, were
among the happiest of his life. Besides trying his best
to set himself to farm-industry, he was otherwise bent on
well-doing. He had, soon after his arrival in Ellisland,
started a parish library, both for his own use and to
spread a love of literature among his neighbours, the
portioners and peasants of Dunscore. When he first took
up house at Ellisland, he used every evening when he was

at home, to gather his household for family worship, and, after the old Scottish custom, himself to offer up prayer in his own words. He was regular, if not constant, in his attendance at the parish church of Dunscore, in which a worthy minister, Mr. Kirkpatrick, officiated, whom he respected for his character, though he sometimes demurred to what seemed to him the too great sternness of his doctrine.

Burns and his wife had not been long settled in their newly - built farm - house, when prudence induced him to ask that he might be appointed Excise officer in the district in which he lived. This request Mr. Graham of Fintray, who had placed his name on the Excise list before he left Edinburgh, at once granted. The reasons that impelled Burns to this step were the increase of his family by the birth of a son in August, 1789, and the prospect that his second year's harvest would be a failure like the first. He often repeats that it was solely to make provision for his increasing family that he submitted to the degradation of—

> "Searching auld wives' barrels—
>   Och, hon! the day!
> That clarty barm should stain my laurels,
>   But—what 'ill ye say?
> These movin things, ca'd wives and weans,
> Wad move the very hearts o' stanes."

That he felt keenly the slur that attached to the name of gauger is certain, but it is honourable to him that he resolved bravely to endure it for the sake of his family.

"I know not," he writes, "how the word exciseman, or the still more opprobrious gauger, will sound in your ears. I, too, have seen the day when my auditory nerves would have felt very delicately on this subject; but a wife and

children are things which have a wonderful power in
blunting this kind of sensations. Fifty pounds a year
for life, and a provision for widows and orphans, you will
allow, is no bad settlement for a poet."

In announcing to Dr. Blacklock his new employment,
he says—

> "But what d'ye think, my trusty fier,
> I'm turned a gauger—Peace be here!
> Parnassian queans, I fear, I fear,
>   Ye'll now disdain me!
> And then my fifty pounds a year
>   Will little gain me.
>
>   *   *   *   *   *
>
> "Ye ken, ye ken
> That strang necessity supreme is
>   'Mang sons o' men.
> I hae a wife and twa wee laddies,
> They maun hae brose and brats o' duddies;
> Ye ken yoursels my heart right proud is,
>   I need na vaunt,
> But I'll sned besoms, thraw saugh woodies,
>   Before they want."

He would cut brooms and twist willow-ropes before his
children should want. But perhaps, as the latest editor of
Burns's poems observes, his best saying on the subject of
the excisemanship was that word to Lady Glencairn, the
mother of his patron, "I would much rather have it said
that my profession borrowed credit from me, than that I
borrowed it from my profession."

In these words we see something of the bitterness about
his new employment, which often escaped from him, both
in prose and verse. Nevertheless, having undertaken it,
he set his face honestly to the work. He had to survey
ten parishes, covering a tract of not less than fifty miles
each way, and requiring him to ride two hundred miles

a week. Smuggling was then common throughout Scotland, both in the shape of brewing and of selling beer and whiskey without licence. Burns took a serious yet humane view of his duty. To the regular smuggler he is said to have been severe; to the country folk, farmers or cotters, who sometimes transgressed, he tempered justice with mercy. Many stories are told of his leniency to these last. At Thornhill, on a fair day, he was seen to call at the door of a poor woman who for the day was doing a little illicit business on her own account. A nod and a movement of the forefinger brought the woman to the doorway. "Kate, are you mad? Don't you know that the supervisor and I will be in upon you in forty minutes?" Burns at once disappeared among the crowd, and the poor woman was saved a heavy fine. Another day the poet and a brother gauger entered a widow's house at Dunscore and seized a quantity of smuggled tobacco. "Jenny," said Burns, "I expected this would be the upshot. Here, Lewars, take note of the number of rolls as I count them. Now, Jock, did you ever hear an auld wife numbering her threads before check-reels were invented? Thou's ane, and thou's no ane, and thou's ane a'out — listen." As he handed out the rolls, and numbered them, old-wife fashion, he dropped every other roll into Jenny's lap. Lewars took the desired note with becoming gravity, and saw as though he saw not. Again, a woman who had been brewing, on seeing Burns coming with another exciseman, slipped out by the back door, leaving a servant and a little girl in the house. "Has there been ony brewing for the fair here the day?" "O no, sir, we hae nae licence for that," answered the servant maid. "That's no true," exclaimed the child; "the muckle black kist is fou' o' the bottles o' yill that my

mither sat up a' nicht brewing for the fair." . . . " We are
in a hurry just now," said Burns, " but when we return
from the fair, we'll examine the muckle black kist." In
acts like these, and in many another anecdote that might be
given, is seen the genuine human-heartedness of the man,
in strange contrast with the bitternesses which so often
find vent in his letters. Ultimately, as we shall see, the
exciseman's work told heavily against his farming, his
poetry, and his habits of life. But it was some time before this became apparent. The solitary rides through
the moors and dales that border Nithsdale gave him opportunities, if not for composing long poems, at any rate
for crooning over those short songs in which mainly his
genius now found vent. " The visits of the muses to me,"
he writes, " and I believe to most of their acquaintance,
like the visits of good angels, are short and far between ;
but I meet them now and then as I jog through the hills
of Nithsdale, just as I used to do on the banks of Ayr."

Take as a sample some of the varying moods he passed
through in the summer and autumn of 1789. In the
May-time of that year an incident occurs, which the poet
thus describes :—" One morning lately, as I was out pretty early in the fields, sowing some grass-seeds, I heard the
burst of a shot from a neighbouring plantation, and presently a poor little wounded hare came hirpling by me.
You will guess my indignation at the inhuman fellow who
could shoot a hare at this season, when all of them have
young ones. Indeed, there is something in the business of
destroying, for our sport, individuals in the animal creation that do not injure us materially, which I could never
reconcile to my ideas of virtue." The lad who fired the
shot and roused the poet's indignation, was the son of a
neighbouring farmer. Burns cursed him, and, being near

the Nith at the time, threatened to throw him into the
river. He found, however, a more innocent vent for his
feelings in the following lines:

> "Inhuman man! curse on thy barbarous art,
>   And blasted be thy murder-aiming eye!
>   May never pity soothe thee with a sigh,
> Nor ever pleasure glad thy cruel heart!
>
> "Go live, poor wanderer of the wood and field,
>   The bitter little that of life remains:
>   No more the thickening brakes and verdant plains
> To thee shall home, or food, or pastime yield.
>
> "Seek, mangled wretch, some place of wonted rest,
>   No more of rest, but now thy dying bed!
>   The sheltering rushes whistling o'er thy head,
> The cold earth with thy bloody bosom prest.
>
> "Perhaps a mother's anguish adds its woe;
>   The playful pair crowd fondly by thy side;
>   Ah! helpless nurslings, who will now provide
> That life a mother only can bestow!
>
> "Oft as by winding Nith, I, musing, wait
>   The sober eve, or hail the cheerful dawn,
>   I'll miss thee sporting o'er the dewy lawn,
> And curse the ruffian's aim, and mourn thy hapless fate."

This, which is one of the best of the very few good poems
which Burns composed in classical English, is no mere sentimental effusion, but expresses what in him was a real part
of his nature—his tender feeling towards his lower fellow-
creatures. The same feeling finds expression in the lines
on *The Mouse, The Auld Farmer's Address to his Mare*,
and *The Winter Night*, when, as he sits by his fireside, and
hears the storm roaring without, he says—

> "I thought me on the ourie cattle,
>   Or silly sheep, wha bide this brattle

> O' wintry war.
> Or thro' the drift, deep-lairing, sprattle,
>   Beneath a scaur.
> Ilk happing bird, wee helpless thing,
> That in the merry months o' spring
> Delighted me to hear thee sing,
>   What comes o' thee?
> Whare wilt thou cow'r thy chittering wing,
>   And close thy e'e?"

Though for a time, influenced by the advice of critics,
Burns had tried to compose some poems according to the
approved models of book-English, we find him presently
reverting to his own Doric, which he had lately too much
abandoned, and writing in good broad Scotch his admira-
bly humorous description of Captain Grose, an Antiquary,
whom he had met at Friars Carse:

> "Hear, Land o' Cakes, and brither Scots,
>   Frae Maidenkirk to Johnnie Groats—
> If there's a hole in a' your coats,
>   I rede you tent it:
> A chield's amang you, takin' notes,
>   And, faith, he'll prent it.

> "By some auld, houlet-haunted biggin,
>   Or kirk deserted by its riggin,
> It's ten to ane ye'll find him snug in
>   Some eldritch part,
> Wi' deils, they say, Lord save's! colleaguin'
>   At some black art.

> "It's tauld he was a sodger bred,
>   And ane wad rather fa'n than fled;
> But now he's quat the spurtle-blade,
>   And dog-skin wallet,
> And taen the—Antiquarian trade,
>   I think they call it.

> " He has a fouth o' auld nick-nackets;
>   Rusty airn caps, and jinglin' jackets,
>   Wad haud the Lothians three in tackets,
>   A towmont gude
>   And parritch-pats and auld saut-backets,
>   Before the Flood.

>   *   *   *   *

> " Forbye, he'll shape you aff fu' gleg
>   The cut of Adam's philibeg;
>   The knife that nicket Abel's craig
>   He'll prove you fully,
>   It was a faulding jocteleg
>   Or lang-kail gullie."

The meeting with Captain Grose took place in the summer of 1789, and the stanzas just given were written probably about the same time. To the same date belongs his ballad called *The Kirk's Alarm*, in which he once more reverts to the defence of one of his old friends of the New Light school, who had got into the Church Courts, and was in jeopardy from the attacks of his more orthodox brethren. The ballad in itself has little merit, except as showing that Burns still clung to the same school of divines to which he had early attached himself. In September we find him writing in a more serious strain to Mrs. Dunlop, and suggesting thoughts which might console her in some affliction under which she was suffering. ". . . In vain would we reason and pretend to doubt. I have myself done so to a very daring pitch; but when I reflected that I was opposing the most ardent wishes and the most darling hopes of good men, and flying in the face of all human belief, in all ages, I was shocked at my own conduct."

That same September, Burns, with his friend Allan Masterton, crossed from Nithsdale to Annandale to visit their

common friend Nicol, who was spending his vacation in
Moffatdale.   They met and spent a night in Nicol's lodging.   It was a small thatched cottage, near Craigieburn—
a place celebrated by Burns in one of his songs—and
stands on the right-hand side as the traveller passes up
Moffatdale to Yarrow, between the road and the river.
Few pass that way now without having the cottage pointed out as the place where the three merry comrades met
that night.

"We had such a joyous meeting," Burns writes, "that
Mr. Masterton and I agreed, each in our own way, that we
should celebrate the business," and Burns's celebration of
it was the famous bacchanalian song—

> "O, Willie brewed a peck o' maut,
>   And Rob and Allan cam to pree."

If bacchanalian songs are to be written at all, this certainly must be pronounced "The king amang them a'."   But
while no one can withhold admiration from the genius and
inimitable humour of the song, still we read it with very
mingled feelings, when we think that perhaps it may have
helped some topers since Burns's day a little faster on the
road to ruin.   As for the three boon-companions themselves, just ten years after that night, Currie wrote, "These
three honest fellows—all men of uncommon talents—are
now all under the turf."   And in 1821, John Struthers, a
Scottish poet little known, but of great worth and some
genius, thus recurs to Currie's words:—

> "Nae mair in learning Willie toils, nor Allan wakes the melting lay,
>   Nor Rab, wi' fancy-witching wiles, beguiles the hour o' dawning
>   day;
>   For tho' they were na very fou, that wicked wee drap in the e'e
>   Has done its turn; untimely now the green grass waves o'er a'
>   the three."

Willie brewed a Peck o' Maut was soon followed by another bacchanalian effusion, the ballad called *The Whistle*. Three lairds, all neighbours of Burns at Ellisland, met at Friars Carse on the 16th of October, 1789, to contend with each other in a drinking-bout. The prize was an ancient ebony whistle, said to have been brought to Scotland in the reign of James the Sixth by a Dane, who, after three days and three nights' contest in hard drinking, was overcome by Sir Robert Laurie, of Maxwelton, with whom the whistle remained as a trophy. It passed into the Riddell family, and now in Burns's time it was to be again contested for in the same rude orgie. Burns was appointed the bard to celebrate the contest. Much discussion has been carried on by his biographers as to whether Burns was present or not. Some maintain that he sat out the drinking-match, and shared the deep potations. Others, and among these his latest editor, Mr. Scott Douglas, maintain that he was not present that night in body, but only in spirit. Anyhow, the ballad remains a monument, if not of his genius, at least of his sympathy with that ancient but now happily exploded form of good fellowship.

This "mighty claret-shed at the Carse," and the ballad commemorative of it, belong to the 16th of October, 1789. It must have been within a few days of that merry-meeting that Burns fell into another and very different mood, which has recorded itself in an immortal lyric. It would seem that from the year 1786 onwards, a cloud of melancholy generally gathered over the poet's soul toward the end of each autumn. This October, as the anniversary of Highland Mary's death drew on, he was observed by his wife to "grow sad about something, and to wander solitary on the banks of Nith, and about his farm-yard, in the extremest agitation of mind nearly the whole night. He

screened himself on the lee-side of a corn-stack from the
cutting edge of the night wind, and lingered till approaching dawn wiped out the stars, one by one, from the firma-
ment." Some more details Lockhart has added, said to
have been received from Mrs. Burns, but these the latest
editor regards as mythical. However this may be, it would
appear that it was only after his wife had frequently en-
treated him, that he was persuaded to return to his home,
where he sat down and wrote, as they now stand, these pathetic lines:

> "Thou lingering star, with lessening ray,
>   That lovest to greet the early morn,
> Again thou usherest in the day
>   My Mary from my soul was torn.
> O Mary! dear departed shade!
>   Where is thy place of blissful rest?
> See'st thou thy lover lowly laid?
>   Hear'st thou the groans that rend his breast?"

That Burns should have expressed, in such rapid succession, the height of drunken revelry in *Willie brewed a
Peck o' Maut* and in the ballad of *The Whistle,* and then
the depth of despondent regret in the lines *To Mary in
Heaven,* is highly characteristic of him. To have many
moods belongs to the poetic nature, but no poet ever passed more rapidly than Burns from one pole of feeling to
its very opposite. Such a poem as this last could not
possibly have proceeded from any but the deepest and
most genuine feeling. Once again, at the same season,
three years later (1792), his thoughts went back to Highland Mary, and he poured forth his last sad wail for her in
the simpler, not less touching song, beginning—

> "Ye banks, and braes, and streams around
>   The castle o' Montgomery!

Green be your woods, and fair your flowers,
 Your waters never drumlie;
There simmer first unfauld her robes,
 And there the langest tarry;
For there I took the last Fareweel
 O' my sweet Highland Mary."

It would seem as though these retrospects were always accompanied by special despondency. For, at the very time he composed this latter song, he wrote thus to his faithful friend, Mrs. Dunlop:

" Alas! who would wish for many years? What is it but to drag existence until our joys gradually expire, and leave us in a night of misery, like the gloom which blots out the stars, one by one, from the face of heaven, and leaves us without a ray of comfort in the howling waste?"

To fits of hypochondria and deep dejection he had, as he himself tells us, been subject from his earliest manhood, and he attributes to overtoil in boyhood this tendency which was probably a part of his natural temperament. To a disposition like his, raptures, exaltations, agonies, came as naturally as a uniform neutral-tinted existence to more phlegmatic spirits. But we may be sure that every cause of self-reproach which his past life had stored up in his memory tended to keep him more and more familiar with the lower pole in that fluctuating scale.

Besides these several poems which mark the variety of moods which swept over him during the summer and autumn of 1789, there was also a continual succession of songs on the anvil in preparation for *Johnson's Museum.* This work of song-making, begun during his second winter in Edinburgh, was carried on with little intermission during all the Ellisland period. The songs were on all kinds of subjects, and of all degrees of excellence, but hardly one, even the most trivial, was without some small touch which could have come from no hand but that of Burns. Sometimes they were old songs with a stanza or two added. Oftener an old chorus or single line was taken up, and made the hint out of which a new and original song was woven. At other times they were entirely original both in subject and in expression, though cast in the form of the ancient minstrelsy. Among so many and so rapidly succeeding efforts, it was only now and then, when a happier moment of inspiration was granted him, that there came forth one song of supreme excellence, perfect alike in conception and in expression. The consummate song of this summer (1789) was *John Anderson my Joe, John,* just as *Auld Lang Syne* and *The Silver Tassie* had been those of the former year.

During the remainder of the year 1789 Burns seems to have continued more or less in the mood of mind indicated by the lines *To Mary in Heaven.* He was suffering from nervous derangement, and this, as usual with him, made him despondent. This is the way in which he writes to Mrs. Dunlop on the 13th December, 1789:

"I am groaning under the miseries of a diseased nervous system—a system, the state of which is most conducive to our happiness, or the most productive of our misery. For now near three weeks I have been so ill with a nervous headache, that I have been obliged for a time to give up my Excise-books, being scarce able to lift my head, much less to ride once a week over ten muir parishes. What is man? . . ."

And then he goes on to moralize in a half-believing, half-doubting kind of way, on the probability of a life to come, and ends by speaking of, or rather apostrophizing, Jesus Christ in a strain which would seem to savour of Socinianism. This letter he calls "a distracted scrawl which the writer dare scarcely read." And yet it appears to have been deliberately copied with some amplification from an entry in his last year's commonplace-book. Even the few passages from his correspondence already given are enough to show that there was in Burns's letter-writing something strained and artificial. But such discoveries as this seem to reveal an extent of effort, and even of artifice, which one would hardly otherwise have guessed at.

In the same strain of harassment as the preceding extract, but pointing to another and more definite cause of it, is the following, written on the 20th December, 1789, to Provost Maxwell of Lochmaben:

"My poor distracted mind is so torn, so jaded, so racked and bedevilled with the task of the superlatively damned, to make one guinea do the business of three, that I detest, abhor, and swoon at the very word business, though no less than four letters of my very short surname are in it." The rest of the letter goes off in a wild rollicking strain, inconsistent enough with his more serious thoughts. But the part of it above given points to a very real reason for his growing discontent with Ellisland.

By the beginning of 1790 the hopelessness of his farming prospects pressed on him still more heavily, and formed one ingredient in the mental depression with which he saw a new year dawn. Whether he did wisely in attempting the Excise business, who shall now say? In one respect it seemed a substantial gain. But this gain was accompanied by counterbalancing disadvantages. The new duties more and more withdrew him from the farm, which, in order to give it any chance of paying, required not only the aid of the master's hand, but the undivided oversight of the master's eye. In fact, farming to profit and Excise-work were incompatible, and a very few months' trial must have convinced Burns of this. But besides rendering regular farm industry impossible, the weekly absences from home, which his new duties entailed, had other evil consequences. They brought with them continual mental distraction, which forbade all sustained poetic effort, and laid him perilously open to indulgences which were sure to undermine regular habits and peace of mind. About this time (the beginning of 1790), we begin to hear of frequent visits to Dumfries on Excise business, and of protracted lingerings at a certain *howff*, place of resort, called the Globe Tavern, which boded no good. There were also intromissions with a certain company of players then resident in Dumfries, and writings of such prologues for their second-rate pieces, as many a penny-a-liner could have done to order as well. Political ballads, too, came from his pen, siding with this or that party in local elections, all which things as we read, we feel as if we saw some noble high-bred racer harnessed to a dust-cart.

His letters during the first half of 1790 betoken the same restless, unsatisfied spirit as those written towards the end of the previous year. Only we must be on our guard against interpreting his real state of mind too exclusively from his letters. For it seems to have been his habit when writing to his friends to take one mood of mind, which happened to be uppermost in him for the moment, and with which he knew that his correspondent sympathized, and to dwell on this so exclusively that for the moment it filled his whole mental horizon, and shut out every other thought. And not this only, which is the tendency of all ardent and impulsive natures, but we cannot altogether excuse Burns of at times half-consciously exaggerating these momentary moods, almost for certain

stage effects which they produced. It is necessary, therefore, in estimating his real condition at any time, to set
against the account, which he gives of himself in his letters, the evidence of other facts, such as the testimony of
those who met him from time to time, and who have left
some record of those interviews. This I shall now do for
the first half of the year 1790, and shall place, over against
his self-revelations, some observations which show how he
at this time appeared to others.

An intelligent man named William Clark, who had served
Burns as a ploughman at Ellisland during the winter half-
year of 1789–90, survived till 1838, and in his old age
gave this account of his former master: "Burns kept two
men and two women servants, but he invariably when at
home took his meals with his wife and family in the little parlour." Clark thought he was as good a manager of
land as most of the farmers in the neighbourhood. The
farm of Ellisland was moderately rented, and was suscepti-
ble of much improvement, had improvement been then in
repute. Burns sometimes visited the neighbouring farmers, and they returned the compliment; but that way of
spending time was not so common then as now. No one
thought that the poet and his writings would be so much
noticed afterwards. He kept nine or ten milch cows, some
young cattle, four horses, and several pet sheep: of the
latter he was very fond. During the winter and spring-
time, when not engaged in Excise business, "he sometimes
held the plough for an hour or two for him (W. Clark),
and was a fair workman. During seed-time, Burns might
be frequently seen at an early hour in the fields with his
sowing sheet; but as he was often called away on business,
he did not sow the whole of his grain."

This old man went on to describe Burns as a kindly and

indulgent master, who spoke familiarly to his servants, both at home and a-field; quick-tempered when anything put him out, but quickly pacified. Once only Clark saw him really angry, when one of the lasses had nearly choked one of the cows by giving her potatoes not cut small enough. Burns's looks, gestures, and voice were then terrible. Clark slunk out of the way, and when he returned, his master was quite calm again. When there was extra work to be done, he would give his servants a dram, but he was by no means *over-flush* in this way. During the six months of his service, Clark never once saw Burns intoxicated or incapable of managing his business. The poet, when at home, used to wear a broad blue bonnet, a long-tailed coat, drab or blue, corduroy breeches, dark blue stockings, with *cootikens* or gaiters. In cold weather he would have a plaid of black and white check wrapped round his shoulders. The same old man describes Mrs. Burns as a good and prudent housewife, keeping everything neat and tidy, well liked by her servants, for whom she provided good and abundant fare. When they parted, Burns paid Clark his wages in full, gave him a written character, and a shilling for a *fairing*.

In the summer or autumn of the same year the scholarly Ramsay of Ochtertyre in the course of a tour looked in on Burns, and here is the record of his visit which Ramsay gave in a letter to Currie. "Seeing him pass quickly near Closeburn, I said to my companion, 'That is Burns.' On coming to the inn, the hostler told us he would be back in a few hours to grant permits; that where he met with anything seizable, he was no better than any other gauger; in everything else that he was perfectly a gentleman. After leaving a note to be delivered to him on his return, I proceeded to his house, being curious to see his

Jean. I was much pleased with his 'uxor Sabina qualis,' and the poet's modest mansion, so unlike the habitation of ordinary rustics. In the evening he suddenly bounced in upon us, and said, as he entered, 'I come, to use the words of Shakespeare, *stewed in haste*.' In fact, he had ridden incredibly fast after receiving my note. We fell into conversation directly, and soon got into the *mare magnum* of poetry. He told me he had now gotten a subject for a drama, which he was to call *Rob McQuech-an's Elshin*, from a popular story of Robert Bruce being defeated on the water of Cairn, when the heel of his boot having loosened in his flight, he applied to Robert Mac-Quechan to fit it, who, to make sure, ran his awl nine inches up the king's heel. We were now going on at a great rate, when Mr. Stewart popped in his head, which put a stop to our discourse, which had become very interesting. Yet in a little while it was resumed, and such was the force and versatility of the bard's genius, that he made the tears run down Mr. Stewart's cheeks, albeit unused to the poetic strain. From that time we met no more, and I was grieved at the reports of him afterwards. Poor Burns! we shall hardly ever see his like again. He was, in truth, a sort of comet in literature, irregular in its motions, which did no good, proportioned to the blaze of light it displayed."

It seems that during this autumn there came a momentary blink in Burns's clouded sky, a blink which, alas! never brightened into full sunshine. He had been but a year in the Excise employment, when, through the renewed kindness of Mr. Graham of Fintray, there seemed a near prospect of his being promoted to a supervisorship, which would have given him an income of 200*l*. a year. So probable at the time did it seem, that his friend Nicol wrote to Ainslie expressing some fears that the poet might

turn his back on his old friends when to the pride of applauded genius was added the pride of office and income.
This may have been ironical on Nicol's part, but he might
have spared his irony on his friend, for the promotion
never came.

But what had Burns been doing for the last year in
poetic production? In this respect the whole interval between the composition of the lines *To Mary in Heaven*,
in October, 1789, and the autumn of the succeeding year,
is almost a blank. Three electioneering ballads, besides a
few trivial pieces, make up the whole. There is not a line
written by him during this year which, if it were deleted
from his works, would anyway impair his poetic fame.
But this long barrenness was atoned for by a burst of
inspiration which came on him in the fall of 1790, and
struck off at one heat the matchless *Tale of Tam o' Shanter*. It was to the meeting already noticed of Burns with
Captain Grose, the antiquary, at Friars Carse, that we owe
this wonderful poem. The poet and the antiquary suited
each other exactly, and they soon became

"Unco pack and thick thegither."

Burns asked his friend, when he reached Ayrshire, to make
a drawing of Alloway kirk, and include it in his sketches,
for it was dear to him because it was the resting-place of
his father, and there he himself might some day lay his
bones. To induce Grose to do this, Burns told him that
Alloway kirk was the scene of many witch stories and
weird sights. The antiquary replied, "Write you a poem
on the scene, and I'll put in the verses with an engraving
of the ruin." Burns having found a fitting day and hour,
when "his barmy noddle was working prime," walked out
to his favourite path down the western bank of the river.

The poem was the work of one day, of which Mrs. Burns
retained a vivid recollection. Her husband had spent most
of the day by the river side, and in the afternoon she joined him with her two children. He was busily engaged
crooning to himsel; and Mrs. Burns, perceiving that her
presence was an interruption, loitered behind with her little ones among the broom. Her attention was presently
attracted by the strange and wild gesticulations of the
bard, who was now seen at some distance, agonized with
an ungovernable access of joy. He was reciting very loud,
and with tears rolling down his cheeks, those animated
verses which he had just conceived—

> "Now Tam! O Tam! had thae been queans,
>   A' plump and strappin' in their teens."

"I wish ye had seen him," said his wife; "he was in
such ecstasy that the tears were happing down his cheeks."
These last words are given by Allan Cunningham, in addi-
tion to the above account, which Lockhart got from a man-
uscript journal of Cromek. The poet having committed
the verses to writing on the top of his sod-dyke above the
water, came into the house, and read them immediately in
high triumph at the fireside.

Thus in the case of two of Burns's best poems, we have
an account of the bard as he appeared in his hour of inspiration, not to any literary friend bent on pictorial effect,
but from the plain narrative of his simple and admiring
wife. Burns speaks of *Tam o' Shanter* as his first attempt at a tale in verse—unfortunately it was also his last.
He himself regarded it as his master-piece of all his poems,
and posterity has not, I believe, reversed the judgment.

In this, one of his happiest flights, Burns's imagination
bore him from the vale of Nith back to the banks of

6*

Doon, and to the weird tales he had there heard in childhood, told by the winter firesides. The characters of the
poem have been identified; that of Tam is taken from a
farmer, Douglas Graham, who lived at the farm of Shanter, in the parish of Kirkoswald. He had a scolding wife,
called Helen McTaggart, and the tombstones of both are
pointed out in Kirkoswald kirkyard. Souter Johnnie is
more uncertain, but is supposed, with some probability, to
have been John Davidson, a shoemaker, who lies buried in
the same place. Yet, from Burns's poem we would gather
that this latter lived in Ayr. But these things matter little. From his experience of the smuggling farmers of
Kirkoswald, among whom "he first became acquainted
with scenes of swaggering and riot," and his remembrance
of the tales that haunted the spot where he passed his
childhood, combined with his knowledge of the peasantry,
their habits and superstitions, Burns's imagination wove
the inimitable tale.

After this, the best poetic offspring of the Ellisland
period, Burns composed only a few short pieces during
his tenancy of that farm. Among these, however, was one
which cannot be passed over. In January, 1791, the Earl
of Glencairn, who had been his first, and it may be almost
said, his only real friend and patron among the Scottish
peerage, died at the early age of forty-two, just as he returned to Falmouth after a vain search for health abroad.
Burns had always loved and honoured Lord Glencairn, as
well he might—although his lordship's gentleness had not
always missed giving offence to the poet's sensitive and
proud spirit. Yet, on the whole, he was the best patron
whom Burns had found, or was ever to find among his
countrymen. When then he heard of the earl's death, he
mourned his loss as that of a true friend, and poured forth

a fine lament, which concludes with the following well-known lines:

> "The bridegroom may forget the bride,
>   Was made his wedded wife yestreen;
> The monarch may forget the crown,
>   That on his head an hour has been;
> The mother may forget the child,
>   That smiles sae sweetly on her knee;
> But I'll remember thee, Glencairn,
>   And a' that thou hast done for me."

Burns's elegies, except when they are comical, are not among his happiest efforts. Some of them are frigid and affected. But this was the genuine language of sincere grief. He afterwards showed the permanence of his affection by calling one of his boys James Glencairn.

A few songs make up the roll of the Ellisland productions during 1791. One only of these is noteworthy—that most popular song, *The Banks o' Doon*. His own words in sending it to a friend are these:—"March, 1791. While here I sit, sad and solitary, by the side of a fire, in a little country inn, and drying my wet clothes, in pops a poor fellow of a sodger, and tells me he is going to Ayr. By heavens! say I to myself, with a tide of good spirits, which the magic of that sound, 'Auld Toon o' Ayr,' conjured up, I will send my last song to Mr. Ballantine."

Then he gives the second and best version of the song, beginning thus:

> "Ye flowery banks o' bonnie Doon,
>   How can ye blume sae fair?
> How can ye chant, ye little birds,
>   And I sae fu' o' care!"

The latest edition of Burns's works, by Mr. Scott Douglas, gives three different versions of this song. Any one who will compare these, will see the truth of that remark of the poet, in one of his letters to Dr. Moore, "I have no doubt that the knack, the aptitude to learn the Muses' trade is a gift bestowed by Him who forms the secret bias of the soul; but I as firmly believe that excellence in the profession is the fruit of industry, attention, labour, and pains; at least I am resolved to try my doctrine by the test of experience."

The second version was that which Burns wrought out by careful revision, from an earlier one. Compare, for instance, with the verse given above, the first verse as originally struck off:

> "Sweet are the banks, the banks of Doon,
>   The spreading flowers are fair,
> And everything is blythe and glad,
>   But I am fu' of care."

And the other changes he made on the first draught are all in the way of improvement. It is painful to know, on the authority of Allan Cunningham, that he who composed this pure and perfect song, and many another such, sometimes chose to work in baser metal, and that songware of a lower kind escaped from his hands into the press, and could never afterwards be recalled.

When Burns told Dr. Moore that he was resolved to try by the test of experience the doctrine that good and permanent poetry could not be composed without industry and pains, he had in view other and wider plans of composition than any which he ever realized. He told Ramsay of Ochtertyre, as we have seen, that he had in view to render into poetry a tradition he had found of an adventure in humble life which Bruce met with during his wanderings. Whether he ever did more than think over the

story of Rob McQuechan's Elshin, or into what poetic form
he intended to cast it, we know not. As Sir Walter said,
any poem he might have produced on this subject would
certainly have wanted that tinge of chivalrous feeling which
the manners of the age and the character of the king alike
demanded. But with Burns's ardent admiration of Bruce,
and that power of combining the most homely and humorous incidents with the pathetic and the sublime, which he
displayed in *Tam o' Shanter*, we cannot but regret that he
never had the leisure and freedom from care which would
have allowed him to try his hand on a subject so entirely
to his mind.

Besides this, he had evidently, during his sojourn at Ellisland, meditated some large dramatic attempt. He wrote to
one of his correspondents that he had set himself to study
Shakespeare, and intended to master all the greatest drama-
tists, both of England and France, with a view to a dramatic
effort of his own. If he had attempted it in pure English,
we may venture to predict that he would have failed. But
had he allowed himself that free use of the Scottish dialect
of which he was the supreme master, especially if he had
shaped the subject into a lyrical drama, no one can say
what he might not have achieved. Many of his smaller
poems show that he possessed the genuine dramatic vein.
The Jolly Beggars, unpleasant as from its grossness it is,
shows the presence of this vein in a very high degree, seeing that from materials so unpromising he could make so
much. As Mr. Lockhart has said, "That extraordinary
sketch, coupled with his later lyrics in a higher vein, is
enough to show that in him we had a master capable of
placing the musical drama on a level with the loftiest of
our classical forms."

Regrets have been expressed that Burns, instead of addressing himself to these high poetic enterprises, which had certainly hovered before him, frittered away so much of his time in composing for musical collections a large number of songs, the very abundance of which must have lessened their quality. And yet it may be doubted whether this urgent demand for songs, made on him by Johnson and Thomson, was not the only literary call to which he would in his circumstances have responded. These calls could be met, by sudden efforts, at leisure moments, when some occasional blink of momentary inspiration came over him. Great poems necessarily presuppose that the original inspiration is sustained by concentrated purpose and long-sustained effort; mental habits, which to a nature like Burns's must have at all times been difficult, and which his circumstances during his later years rendered simply impossible. From the first he had seen that his farm would not pay, and each succeeding year confirmed him in this conviction. To escape what he calls "the crushing grip of poverty, which, alas! I fear, is less or more fatal to the worth and purity of the noblest souls," he had, within a year after entering Ellisland, recourse to Excise work. This he did from a stern sense of duty to his wife and family. It was, in fact, one of the most marked instances in which Burns, contrary to his too frequent habit, put pride in his pocket, and sacrificed inclination to duty. But that he had not accepted the yoke without some painful sense of degradation, is shown by the bitterness of many of his remarks, when in his correspondence he alludes to the subject. There were, however, times when he tried to take a brighter view of it, and to persuade himself, as he says in a letter to Lady Harriet Don, that "one advantage he had in this new business was the knowledge it gave him of the various shades of character in man—consequently assisting

him in his trade as a poet." But, alas! whatever advan-
tages in this way it might have brought, were counteracted
tenfold by other circumstances that attended it. The continual calls of a responsible business, itself sufficient to oc-
cupy a man—when divided with the oversight of his farm,
overtasked his powers, and left him no leisure for poetic
work, except from time to time crooning over a random
song. Then the habits which his roving Excise life must
have induced were, even to a soul less social than that of
Burns, perilous in the extreme. The temptations he was
in this way exposed to, Lockhart has drawn with a powerful hand. "From the castle to the cottage, every door
flew open at his approach; and the old system of hospitality, then flourishing, rendered it difficult for the most so-
berly inclined guest to rise from any man's board in the
same trim that he sat down to it. The farmer, if Burns
was seen passing, left his reapers, and trotted by the side
of Jenny Geddes, until he could persuade the bard that the
day was hot enough to demand an extra libation. If he
entered an inn at midnight, after all the inmates were in
bed, the news of his arrival circulated from the cellar to
the garret; and ere ten minutes had elapsed, the landlord
and all his guests were assembled round the ingle; the
largest punch-bowl was produced, and—

　　'Be ours to-night—who knows what comes to-morrow?'

was the language of every eye in the circle that welcomed
him. The highest gentry of the neighbourhood, when bent
on special merriment, did not think the occasion complete
unless the wit and eloquence of Burns were called in to
enliven their carousals."

It can readily be imagined how distracting such a life
must have been, how fatal to all mental concentration on

high objects, not to speak of the habits of which it was
too sure to sow the seeds. The frequent visits to Dumfries which his Excise work entailed, and the haunting of
the Globe Tavern, already spoken of, led to consequences
which, more than even deep potations, must have been
fatal to his peace.

His stay at Ellisland is now hastening to a close. Before passing, however, from that, on the whole the best
period of his life since manhood, one or two incidents of
the spring of 1791 must be mentioned. In the February
of that year Burns received from the Rev. Archibald
Alison, Episcopalian clergyman in Edinburgh, a copy of
his once famous, but now, I believe, forgotten, *Essay on
Taste*, which contained the authorized exposition of that
theory, so congenial to Scotch metaphysics, that objects
seem beautiful to us only because our minds associate
them with sensible objects which have previously given us
pleasure. In his letter to the author, acknowledging the
receipt of his book, Burns says, " I own, sir, at first glance,
several of your propositions startle me as paradoxical :
that the martial clangour of a trumpet had something in
it vastly more grand, heroic, and sublime than the twingle-
twangle of a Jew's-harp ; that the delicate flexure of a
rose-twig, when the half-blown flower is heavy with the
tears of the dawn, was infinitely more beautiful and elegant
than the upright stub of a burdock ; and that from something innate and independent of all association of ideas—
these I had set down as irrefragable orthodox truths until
perusing your book shook my faith." These words so
pierce this soap-bubble of the metaphysicians, that we can
hardly read them without fancying that the poet meant
them to be ironical. Dugald Stewart expressed surprise
that the unschooled Ayrshire ploughman should have

found "a distinct conception of the general principles of the doctrine of association;" on which Mr. Carlyle remarks, "We rather think that far subtler things than the doctrine of association had been of old familiar to him."

In looking over his letters at this time (1791), we are startled by a fierce outburst in one of them, apparently apropos of nothing. He had been recommending to the protection of an Edinburgh friend a schoolmaster, whom he thought unjustly persecuted, when all at once he breaks out : "God help the children of Dependence ! Hated and persecuted by their enemies, and too often, alas ! almost unexceptionally, received by their friends with disrespect and reproach, under the thin disguise of cold civility and humiliating advice. Oh to be a sturdy savage, stalking in the pride of his independence, amid the solitary wilds of his deserts, rather than in civilized life helplessly to tremble for a subsistence, precarious as the caprice of a fellow-creature ! Every man has his virtues, and no man is without his failings ; and curse on that privileged plain-speaking of friendship which, in the hour of my calamity, cannot reach forth the helping-hand without at the same time pointing out those failings, and apportioning them their share in procuring my present distress. . . . I do not want to be independent that I may sin, but I want to be independent in my sinning."

What may have been the cause of this ferocious explosion there is no explanation. Whether the real source of it may not have lain in certain facts which had occurred during the past spring, that must have rudely broken in on the peace at once of his conscience and his home, we cannot say. Certainly it does seem, as Chambers suggests, like one of those sudden outbursts of temper which fasten on some mere passing accident, because the real seat of it

lies too deep for words.   Some instances of the same temper we have already seen.   This is a sample of a growing
exasperation of spirit, which found expression from time
to time till the close of his life.

Let us turn from this painful subject, to one of the only
notices we get of him from a stranger's hand during the
summer of 1791.   Two English gentlemen, who were
travelling, went to visit him; one of whom has left an
amusing account of their reception.   Calling at his house,
they were told that the poet was by the river side, and
thither they went in search of him.   On a rock that pro-
jected into the stream, they saw a man employed in angling, of a singular appearance.   He had a cap of fox's
skin on his head, a loose great-coat fixed round him by a
belt, from which depended an enormous Highland broadsword.   It was Burns.   He received them with great cor-
diality, and asked them to share his humble dinner—an
invitation which they accepted.   " On the table they found
boiled beef, with vegetables and barley broth, after the
manner of Scotland.   After dinner the bard told them
ingenuously that he had no wine, nothing better than
Highland whiskey, a bottle of which he set on the board.
He produced at the same time his punch-bowl, made of
Inverary marble; and, mixing it with water and sugar,
filled their glasses and invited them to drink.   The travellers were in haste, and, besides, the flavour of the whiskey
to their southern palates was scarcely tolerable; but the
generous poet offered them his best, and his ardent hospitality they found impossible to resist.   Burns was in his
happiest mood, and the charm of his conversation was altogether fascinating.   He ranged over a variety of topics,
illuminating whatever he touched.   He related the tales
of his infancy and youth; he recited some of his gayest

and some of his tenderest poems; in the wildest of his strains of mirth he threw in some touches of melancholy, and spread around him the electric emotions of his powerful mind. The Highland whiskey improved in its flavour; the marble bowl was again and again emptied and replenished; the guests of our poet forgot the flight of time and the dictates of prudence; at the hour of midnight they lost their way to Dumfries, and could scarcely distinguish it when assisted by the morning's dawn. There is much naïveté in the way the English visitor narrates his experience of that 'nicht wi' Burns.'"

Mr. Carlyle, if we remember aright, has smiled incredulously at the story of the fox-skin cap, the belt, and the broadsword. But of the latter appendage this is not the only record. Burns himself mentions it as a frequent accompaniment of his when he went out by the river.

The punch-bowl here mentioned is the one which his father-in-law had wrought for him as a marriage-gift. It was, when Chambers wrote his biography of Burns, in the possession of Mr. Haistie, then M.P. for Paisley, who is said to have refused for it three hundred guineas—"a sum," says Chambers, "that would have set Burns on his legs for ever."

This is the last glimpse we get of the poet in his home at Ellisland till the end came. We have seen that he had long determined, if possible, to get rid of his farm. He had sunk in it all the proceeds that remained to him from the sale of the second edition of his poems, and for this the crops he had hitherto reaped had given no adequate return. Three years, however, were a short trial, and there was a good time coming for all farmers, when the war with France broke out, and raised the value of farm produce to a hitherto unknown amount. If Burns could

but have waited for that!—but either he could not, or he
would not wait.   But the truth is, even if Burns ever had
it in him to succeed as a farmer, that time was past when
he came to Ellisland.   Independence at the plough-tail, of
which he often boasted, was no longer possible for him.
He could no more work as he had done of yore.   The
habits contracted in Edinburgh had penetrated too deeply.
Even if he had not been withdrawn from his farm by Excise duties, he could neither work continuously himself,
nor make his servants work.   "Faith," said a neighbouring farmer, "how could he miss but fail?   He brought
with him a bevy of servants from Ayrshire.   The lasses
did nothing but bake bread (that is, oat-cakes), and the
lads sat by the fireside and ate it warm with ale."   Burns
meanwhile enjoying himself at the house of some jovial
farmer or convivial laird.   How could he miss but fail?

When he had resolved on giving up his farm, an arrangement was come to with the Laird of Dalswinton by
which Burns was allowed to throw up his lease and sell
off his crops.   The sale took place in the last week in
August (1791).   Even at this day the auctioneer and the
bottle always appear side by side, as Chambers observes;
but then far more than now-a-days.   After the roup, that
is the sale, of his crop was over, Burns, in one of his letters, describes the scene that took place within and without his house.   It was one which exceeded anything he
had ever seen in drunken horrors.   Mrs. Burns and her
family fortunately were not there to witness it, having
gone many weeks before to Ayrshire, probably to be out
of the way of all the pain that accompanies the breaking
up of a country home.   When Burns gave up his lease,
Mr. Millar, the landlord, sold Ellisland to a stranger, because the farm was an outlying one, inconveniently situ-

ated, on a different side of the river from the rest of his estate. It was in November or December that Burns sold off his farm-stock and implements of husbandry, and moved his family and furniture into the town of Dumfries, leaving at Ellisland no memorial of himself, as Allan Cunningham tells us, "but a putting-stone with which he loved to exercise his strength, and 300l. of his money, sunk beyond redemption in a speculation from which all had augured happiness."

It is not without deep regret that even now we think of Burns's departure from this beautiful spot. If there was any position on earth in which he could have been happy and fulfilled his genius, it would have been on such a farm — always providing that it could have given him the means of a comfortable livelihood, and that he himself could have guided his ways aright. That he might have had a fair opportunity, how often one has wished that he could have met some landlord who could have acted towards him, as the present Duke of Buccleuch did towards the Ettrick Shepherd in his later days, and have given a farm on which he could have sat rent-free. Such an act, one is apt to fancy, would have been honourable alike to giver and receiver. Indeed, a truly noble nature would have been only too grateful to find such an opportunity put in his way of employing a small part of his wealth for so good an end. But the notions of modern society, founded as they are so entirely on individual independence, for the most part preclude the doing and the receiving of such favours. And with this social feeling no man was ever more filled than Burns.

CHAPTER VI.

A GREAT change it must have been to pass from the pleasant holms and broomy banks of the Nith at Ellisland to a town home in the Wee Vennel of Dumfries. It was, moreover, a confession visible to the world of what Burns himself had long felt, that his endeavour to combine the actual and the ideal, his natural calling as a farmer with the exercise of his gift as a poet, had failed, and that henceforth he must submit to a round of toil, which, neither in itself nor in its surroundings, had anything to redeem it from commonplace drudgery. He must have felt, from the time when he first became Exciseman, that he had parted company with all thought of steadily working out his ideal, and that whatever he might now do in that way must be by random snatches. To his proud spirit the name of gauger must have been gall and wormwood, and it is much to his credit that for the sake of his wife and children he was content to undergo what he often felt to be a social obloquy. It would have been well for him if this had been the only drawback to his new calling. Unfortunately the life into which it led him exposed him to those very temptations which his nature was least able to withstand. If social indulgence and irregular habits had somewhat impaired his better resolves, and his power of poetic concentration, before he left Ellisland, Dumfries,

and the society into which it threw him, did with increased
rapidity the fatal work which had been already begun.
His biographers, though with varying degrees of emphasis,
on the whole, agree that, from the time he settled in Dumfries, "his moral course was downwards."

The social condition of Dumfries at the time when
Burns went to live in it was neither better nor worse than
that of other provincial towns in Scotland. What that
was, Dr. Chambers has depicted from his own youthful
experience of just such another country town. The curse
of such towns, he tells us, was that large numbers of their
inhabitants were either half or wholly idle; either men
living on competences, with nothing to do, or shopkeepers
with their time but half employed; their only amusement
to meet in taverns, soak, gossip, and make stupid personal
jokes. "The weary waste of spirits and energy at those
soaking evening meetings was deplorable. Insipid toasts,
petty raillery, empty gabble about trivial occurrences, end-
less disputes on small questions of fact, these relieved now
and then by a song"—such Chambers describes as the
items which made up provincial town life in his younger
days. "A life," he says, "it was without progress or
profit, or anything that tended to moral elevation." For
such dull companies to get a spirit like Burns among
them, to enliven them with his wit and eloquence, what a
windfall it must have been! But for him to put his time
and his powers at their disposal, how great the degradation!
During the day, no doubt, he was employed busily enough
in doing his duty as an Exciseman. This could now be
done with less travelling than in the Ellisland days, and
did not require him, as formerly, to keep a horse. When
the day's work was over, his small house in the Wee
Vennel, and the domestic hearth with the family ties gath-

ered round it, were not enough for him.   At Ellisland he
had sung—

> " To make a happy fire-side clime,
>   For weans and wife,
>   Is the true pathos and sublime
>   Of human life. '

But it is one thing to sing wisely, another to practise
wisdom.   Too frequently at nights Burns's love of sociality and excitement drove him forth to seek the compan-
ionship of neighbours and drouthy cronies, who gathered
habitually at the Globe Tavern and other such haunts.
From these he was always sure to meet a warm welcome,
abundant appreciation, and even flattery, for to this he
was not inaccessible ; while their humble station did not
jar in any way on his social prejudices, nor their mediocre
talents interfere with his love of pre-eminence.   In such
companies Burns no doubt had the gratification of feeling
that he was, what is proverbially called, cock of the walk.
The desire to be so probably grew with that growing dislike to the rich and the titled, which was observed in him
after he came to Dumfries.   In earlier days we have seen
that he did not shrink from the society of the greatest
magnates, and when they showed him that deference
which he thought his due, he even enjoyed it.   But now
so bitter had grown his scorn and dislike of the upper
classes, that we are told that if any one named a lord, or
alluded to a man of rank in his presence, he instantly
"crushed the offender in an epigram, or insulted him by
some sarcastic sally."   In a letter written during his first
year at Dumfries, this is the way he speaks of his daily
occupations :—" Hurry of business, grinding the faces of
the publican and the sinner on the merciless wheels of
the Excise, making ballads, and then drinking and singing

them; and over and above all, correcting the press of two
different publications." But besides these duties by day
and the convivialities by night, there were other calls on
his time and strength, to which Burns was by his reputation exposed. When those of the country gentry whom
he still knew were in Dumfries for some hours, or when
any party of strangers passing through the town had an
idle evening on their hands, it seems to have been their
custom to summon Burns to assist them in spending it;
and he was weak enough, on receiving the message, to
leave his home and adjourn to the Globe, the George, or
the King's Arms, there to drink with them late into the
night, and waste his powers for their amusement. Verily,
a Samson, as has been said, making sport for Philistines!

To one such invitation his impromptu answer was—

> "The king's most humble servant, I
>   Can scarcely spare a minute;
> But I'll be with you by-and-by,
>   Or else the devil's in it."

And this we may be sure was the spirit of many another reply to these ill-omened invitations. It would have
been well if, on these occasions, the pride he boasted of
had stood him in better stead, and repelled such unjustifi-
able intrusions. But in this, as in so many other respects,
Burns was the most inconsistent of men.

From the time of his migration to Dumfries, it would
appear that he was gradually dropped out of an acquaintance by most of the Dumfriesshire lairds, as he had long
been by the parochial and all other ministers. I have
only conversed with one person who remembered in his
boyhood to have seen Burns. He was the son of a Dumfriesshire baronet, the representative of the House of Red-

gauntlet. The poet was frequently in the neighbourhood
of the baronet's country seat, but the old gentleman so
highly disapproved of "Robbie Burns," that he forbade
his sons to have anything to do with him. My inform-
ant, therefore, though he had often seen, had never spoken
to the poet. When I conversed with him, his age was
nigh four-score years, and the one thing he remembered about Burns was "the blink of his black eye."
This is probably but a sample of the feeling with which
Burns was regarded by most of the country gentry around
Dumfries. What were the various ingredients that made
up their dislike of him it is not easy now exactly to determine. Politics most likely had a good deal to do with
it, for they were Tories and aristocrats, Burns was a Whig
and something more. Though politics may have formed
the chief, they were not probably the only element in their
aversion. Yet though the majority of the county families turned their backs on him, there were some with which
he still continued intimate.

These were either the few Whig magnates of the southern counties, whose political projects he supported by electioneering ballads, charged with all the powers of sarcasm
he could wield; or those still fewer, whose literary tastes
were strong enough to make them willing, for the sake of
his genius, to tolerate both his radical politics and his irregular life. Among these latter was a younger brother
of Burns's old friend, Glen Riddel, Mr. Walter Riddel, who
with his wife had settled at a place four miles from Dumfries, formerly called Goldie-lea, but named after Mrs. Riddel's maiden name, Woodley Park. Mrs. Riddel was handsome, clever, witty, not without some tincture of letters,
and some turn for verse-making. She and her husband
welcomed the poet to Woodley Park, where for two years

he was a constant and favourite guest. The lady's wit and literary taste found, it may be believed, no other so responsive spirit in all the south of Scotland. In the third year came a breach in their friendship, followed by a savage lampoon of Burns on the lady, because she did not at once accept his apology; then a period of estrangement. After an interval, however, the Riddels forgave the insult, and were reconciled to the poet, and when the end came, Mrs. Riddel did her best to befriend him, and to do honour to his memory when he was gone.

It ought perhaps to have been mentioned before, that about the time of Burns's first settling at Dumfries, that is towards the close of 1791, he paid his last visit to Edinburgh. It was occasioned by the news that Clarinda was about to sail for the West Indies, in search of the husband who had forsaken her. Since Burns's marriage the silence between them seems to have been broken by only two letters to Clarinda from Ellisland. In the first of these he resents the name of "villain," with which she appears to have saluted him. In the second he admits that his past conduct had been wrong, but concludes by repeating his error and enclosing a song addressed to her in the most exaggerated strain of love. Now he rushed to Edinburgh to see her once more before she sailed. The interview was a brief and hurried one, and no record of it remains, except some letters and a few impassioned lyrics which about that time he addressed to her. The first letter is stiff and formal, as if to break the ice of long estrangement. The others are in the last strain of rapturous devotion—language which, if feigned, is the height of folly; if real, is worse. The lyrics are some of them strained and artificial. One, however, stands out from all the rest, as one of the most impassioned effusions that Burns ever

poured forth.   It contains that one consummate stanza
in which Scott, Byron, and many more, saw concentrated
"the essence of a thousand love-tales"—

> "Had we never loved so kindly,
> Had we never loved so blindly;
> Never met, or never parted,
> We had ne'er been broken-hearted."

After a time Mrs. M'Lehose returned from the West
Indies, but without having recovered her truant husband.
On her return, one or two more letters Burns wrote to her
in the old exaggerated strain—the last in June, 1794—after which Clarinda disappears from the scene.

Other Delilahs on a smaller scale Burns met with during his Dumfries sojourn, and to these he was ever and
anon addressing songs of fancied love.   By the attentions
which the wayward husband was continually paying to
ladies and others into whose society his wife could not
accompany him, the patience of "bonny Jean," it may
easily be conceived, must have been severely tried.

It would have been well, however, if stray flirtations
and Platonic affections had been all that could be laid to
his charge.   But there is a darker story.   The facts of it
are told by Chambers in connexion with the earlier part
of the Dumfries period, and need not be repeated here.
Mrs. Burns is said to have been a marvel of long-suffering
and forgivingness; but the way she bore those wrongs
must have touched her husband's better nature, and pierced
him to the quick.   When his calmer moments came, that
very mildness must have made him feel, as nothing else
could, what self-reproach was, and what

> "Self-contempt bitterer to drink than blood."

To the pangs of that remorse have, I doubt not, been tru-

ly attributed those bitter outpourings of disgust with the
world and with society which are to be found in some of
his letters, especially in those of his later years. Some
samples of these outbreaks have been given; more might
easily have been added. The injuries he may have received from the world and society, what were they compared with those which he could not help feeling that he
had inflicted on himself? It is when a man's own conscience is against him that the world looks worst.

During the first year at Dumfries, Burns for the first
time began to dabble in politics, which ere long landed
him in serious trouble. Before this, though he had passed for a sort of Jacobite, he had been in reality a Whig.
While he lived in Edinburgh he had consorted more with
Whigs than with Tories, but yet he had not in any marked
way committed himself as a partisan. The only exception
to this were some expressions in his poetry favourable to
the Stuarts, and his avowed dislike to the Brunswick dy-
nasty. Yet, notwithstanding these, his Jacobitism was but
skin deep. It was only with him, as with so many another Scot of that day, the expression of his discontent with
the Union of 1707, and his sense of the national degradation that had followed it. When in song he sighed to
see *Jamie come hame*, this was only a sentimental protest
against the existing order of things. But by the time he
came to Dumfries the day of Jacobitism was over, and
the whole aspect of the political heavens seemed dark with
coming change. The French Revolution was in full swing,
and vibrations of it were felt in the remotest corners of
Europe. These reached even to the dull provincial towns
of Scotland, and roused the pot-house politicians with
whom Burns consorted, at the Globe and other taverns, to
unwonted excitement. Under this new stimulus, Burns's

previous Jacobitism passed towards the opposite, but not very distant, extreme of Jacobinism. At these gatherings we may easily imagine that, with his native eloquence, his debating power, trained in the Tarbolton Club, and his ambition to shine as a public speaker, the voice of Burns would be the loudest and most vehement. Liberty, Equality, Fraternity, these were words which must have found an echo in his inmost heart. But it was not only the abstract rights of man, but the concrete wrongs of Scotland that would be there discussed. And wrongs no doubt there were, under which Scotland was suffering, ever since the Union had destroyed not only her nationality, but almost her political existence. The franchise had become very close—in the counties restricted to a few of the chief families—in the boroughs thrown into the hands of the Baillies, who were venal beyond conception. It was the day, too, of Henry Dundas. A prominent member of the Pitt administration, he ruled Scotland as an autocrat, and as the dispenser of all her patronage. A patriotic autocrat no doubt, loving his country, and providing well for those of her people whom he favoured— still an autocrat. The despotism of Dundas has been pictured, in colours we may well believe sufficiently strong, by Lord Cockburn and others bent on inditing the Epic of Whiggery, in which they and their friends should figure as heroes and martyrs. But whatever may be said against Dundas's régime as a permanent system, it must be allowed that this was no time to remodel it when England was face to face with the French troubles. When the tempest is breaking over the ship, the captain may reasonably be excused for thinking that the moment would be ill chosen for renewing cordage or repairing timbers. Whatever may have been right in a time of quiet, it was not unnatural that the Pitt administration should postpone all thoughts of reform, till the vessel of the State had weathered the storm which was then upon her.

Besides his conviction as to public wrongs to be redressed, Burns had, he thought, personal grievances to complain of, which, as is so often seen, added fuel to his reforming zeal. His great powers, which he believed entitled him to a very different position, were unacknowledged and disregarded by the then dispensers of patronage. Once he had been an admirer of Pitt, latterly he could not bear the mention of his name. Of the ministry, Addington, we have seen, was fully alive to his merits, and pressed his claims on Pitt, who himself was quite awake to the charm of Burns's poetry. The Premier, it is said, " pushed the bottle on to Dundas, and did nothing "—to Dundas, too practical and too prosaic to waste a thought on poets and poetry. Latterly this neglect of him by public men preyed on the spirit of Burns, and was seldom absent from his thoughts. It added force, no doubt, to the rapture with which he, like all the younger poets of the time, hailed the French Revolution, and the fancied dawn of that day, which would place plebeian genius and worth in those high places, whence titled emptiness and landed incapacity would be at length thrust ignominiously down.

Burns had not been more than three months in Dumfries, before he found an opportunity of testifying by deed his sympathy with the French Revolutionists. At that time the whole coast of the Solway swarmed with smuggling vessels, carrying on a contraband traffic, and manned by men of reckless character, like the Dirk Hatteraick of *Guy Mannering*. In 1792, a suspicious-looking brig appeared in the Solway, and Burns, with other excisemen,

was set to watch her motions. She got into shallow
water, when the gaugers, enforced by some dragoons,
waded out to her, and Burns, sword in hand, was the first
to board her. The captured brig "Rosamond," with all
her arms and stores, was sold next day at Dumfries, and
Burns became the purchaser of four of her guns. These
he sent, with a letter, to the French Legislative Assembly, requesting them to accept the present as a mark of
his admiration and sympathy. The guns with the letter
never reached their destination. They were, however,
intercepted by the Custom-house officers at Dover, and
Burns at once became a suspected man in the eye of the
Government. Lockhart, who tells this incident, connects
with it the song, *The Deil's awa' wi' the Exciseman*, which
Burns, he said, composed while waiting on the shore to
watch the brig. But Mr. Scott Douglas doubts whether
the song is referable to this occasion. However this may
be, the folly of Burns's act can hardly be disputed. He
was in the employ of Government, and had no right to
express in this way his sympathy with a movement
which, he must have known, the Government, under whom
he served, regarded, if not yet with open hostility, at least
with jealous suspicion. Men who think it part of their
personal right and public duty unreservedly to express, by
word and deed, their views on politics, had better not seek
employment in the public service. Burns having once
drawn upon himself the suspicions of his superiors, all his
words and actions were no doubt closely watched. It was
found that he "gat the Gazetteer," a revolutionary print
published in Edinburgh, which only the most extreme
men patronized, and which after a few months' existence
was suppressed by Government. As the year 1792 drew
to a close, the political heaven, both at home and abroad,

became ominously dark. In Paris the king was in prison,
the Reign of Terror had begun, and innocent blood of
loyalists flowed freely in the streets; the republic which
had been established was threatening to propagate its
principles in other countries by force of arms. In this
country, what at the beginning of the year had been but
suspicion of France, was now turned to avowed hostility,
and war against the republic was on the eve of being
declared. There were uneasy symptoms, too, at home.
Tom Paine's *Rights of Man* and *Age of Reason* were
spreading questionable doctrines and fomenting disaffec-
tion. Societies named Friends of the People were formed
in Edinburgh and the chief towns of Scotland, to demand
reform of the representation and other changes, which,
made at such a time, were believed by those in power to
cover seditious aims. At such a crisis any government
might be expected to see that all its officers, from the
highest to the lowest, were well affected. But though
the Reign of Terror had alarmed many others who had
at first looked favourably on the Revolution in France,
Burns's ardour in its cause was no whit abated. He even
denounced the war on which the ministry had determined;
he openly reviled the men in power; and went so far in
his avowal of democracy that at a social meeting, he proposed as a toast, "Here's the last verse of the last chapter
of the last Book of Kings." This would seem to be but
one specimen of the freedom of political speech in which
Burns at this time habitually indulged—the truculent way
in which he flaunted defiance in the face of authority. It
would not have been surprising if at any time the Government had ordered inquiry to be made into such conduct,
much less in such a season of anxiety and distrust. That
an inquiry was made is undoubted; but as to the result

7*

which followed it, there is uncertainty. Some have
thought that the poet received from his superiors only
a slight hint or caution to be more careful in future.
Others believed, that the matter went so far that he was
in serious danger of dismissal from his post; and that
this was only averted by the timely interposition of some
kind and powerful friends. That Burns himself took a
serious view of it, and was sufficiently excited and alarmed,
may be seen from two letters which he wrote, the one at
the time of the occurrence, the other soon after it. It
was thus that in December, 1792, he addressed Mr. Graham
of Fintray, the same person whose good offices had at first
obtained for the poet his appointment, and whose kindness never failed him while he lived:

"SIR, — I have been surprised, confounded, and distracted by Mr. Mitchell, the collector, telling me that he
has received an order from your Board to inquire into my
political conduct, and blaming me as a person disaffected
to Government.

"Sir, you are a husband and a father. You know what
you would feel to see the much-loved wife of your bosom,
and your helpless, prattling little ones turned adrift into
the world, degraded and disgraced from a situation in
which they had been respectable and respected, and left
almost without the necessary support of a miserable existence.

"Alas! sir, must I think that such soon will be my lot!
and from the dark insinuations of hellish, groundless
envy, too! I believe, sir, I may aver it, and in the sight
of Omniscience, that I would not tell a deliberate false-
hood, no, not though even worse horrors, if worse can be,
than those I have mentioned, hung over my head; and I

say, that the allegation, whatever villain has made it, is a
lie! To the British Constitution, on revolution principles,
next after my God, I am most devoutly attached. You,
sir, have been much and generously my friend.—Heaven
knows how warmly I have felt the obligation, and how
gratefully I have thanked you. Fortune, sir, has made you
powerful, and me impotent—has given you patronage,
and me dependence. I would not, for my single self, call
on your humanity; were such my insular, unconnected
situation, I would despise the tear that now swells in my
eye. I would brave misfortune—I could face ruin, for at
the worst Death's thousand doors stand open; but—the
tender concerns that I have mentioned, the claims and
ties that I see at this moment, and feel around me, how
they unnerve courage and wither resolution! To your
patronage, as a man of some genius, you have allowed me
a claim; and your esteem, as an honest man, I know is
my due. To these, sir, permit me to appeal; by these
may I adjure you to save me from that misery which
threatens to overwhelm me, and which—with my latest
breath I will say it—I have not deserved. R. B."

That this appeal was not without effect may be gathered
from a letter on this same affair, which Burns addressed
on the 13th April, 1793, to Mr. Erskine, of Mar, in which
he says one of the supervisors-general, a Mr. Corbet, "was
instructed to inquire on the spot, and to document me that
my business was to act, *not to think:* and that, whatever
might be men or measures, it was for me to be *silent* and
obedient."

Much obloquy has been heaped upon the Excise Board
—but on what grounds of justice I have never been able
to discover—for the way in which they on this occasion

dealt with Burns. The members of the Board were the
servants of the Government, to which they were responsible for the conduct of all their subordinates. To have allowed any of their subordinates to set themselves up by
word or deed in opposition to the Ministry, and especially
at such a crisis, was inconsistent with the ideas of the time
as to official duty. And when called on to act, it is hard
to see how they could have done so with more leniency
than by hinting to him the remonstrance which so alarmed
and irritated the recipient of it. Whatever may be said
of his alarm, his irritation, if perhaps natural, was not rea-
sonable. No man has a right to expect that, because he
is a genius, he shall be absolved from those rules of conduct, either in private or in public life, which are held
binding on his more commonplace brethren. About the
time when he received this rebuke, he wrote to Mrs. Dunlop, " I have set, henceforth, a seal on my lips as to these
unlucky politics." But neither his own resolve nor the
remonstrance of the Excise Board seem to have weighed
much with him. He continued at convivial parties to express his feelings freely ; and at one of these, shortly after
he had been rebuked by the Excise Board, when the health
of William Pitt was drunk, he followed it by craving a
bumper " to the health of a much better man—General
Washington." And on a subsequent occasion, as we shall
see, he brought himself into trouble by giving an inju-
dicious toast. The repression brought to bear on Burns
cannot have been very stringent when he was still free to
sport such sentiments. The worst effect of the remonstrance he received seems to have been to irritate his temper, and to depress his spirits by the conviction, unfounded
though it was, that all hope of promotion for him was
over.

But amid all the troubles entailed on him by his conduct, domestic, social, and political, the chief refuge and
solace which he found was in exercising his gifts of song.
All hope of his ever achieving a great poem, which called
for sustained effort, was now over. Even poems descriptive of rustic life and characters, such as he had sketched
in his Ayrshire days — for these he had now no longer
either time or inclination. His busy and distracted life,
however, left him leisure from time to time to give vent
to his impulses, or to soothe his feelings by short arrow-
flights of song. He found in his own experience the truth
of those words of another poet—

> "They can make who fail to find
> Short leisure even in busiest days,
> Moments to cast a look behind,
> And profit by those kindly rays
> Which through the clouds will sometimes steal,
> And all the far-off past reveal."

Such breaks in the clouds he eagerly waited for, and
turned every golden gleam to song.

It may be remembered that while Burns was in Edinburgh he became acquainted with James Johnson, who
was engaged in collecting the songs of Scotland in a work
called the *Musical Museum*. He had at once thrown himself ardently into Johnson's undertaking, and put all his
power of traditional knowledge, of criticism, and of original composition at Johnson's disposal. This he continued
to do through all the Ellisland period, and more or less
during his residence in Dumfries. To the *Museum* Burns
from first to last gratuitously contributed not less than
one hundred and eighty-four songs, original, altered, or
collected.

During the first year that Burns lived in Dumfries, in

September, 1792, he received an invitation from Mr. George
Thomson to lend the aid of his lyrical genius to a collection of Scottish melodies, airs, and words, which a small
band of musical amateurs in Edinburgh were then project-
ing.   This collection was pitched to a higher key than the
comparatively humble *Museum.*   It was to be edited with
more rigid care, the symphonies and accompaniments were
to be supplied by the first musicians of Europe, and it was
to be expurgated from all leaven of coarseness, and from
whatever could offend the purest taste.   To Thomson's
proposal Burns at once replied, "As the request you make
to me will positively add to my enjoyment in complying
with it, I shall enter into your undertaking with all the
small portion of abilities I have, strained to their utmost
exertion by the impulse of enthusiasm. . . .

"If you are for English verses, there is, on my part, an
end of the matter.   Whether in the simplicity of the ballad, or the pathos of the song, I can only hope to please
myself in being allowed at least a sprinkling of our native
tongue. . . .   As to remuneration, you may think my songs
either above or below price ; for they shall be absolutely
the one or the other.   In the honest enthusiasm with which
I embark in your undertaking, to talk of money, wages, fee,
hire, &c., would be downright prostitution of soul."

In this spirit he entered on the enterprise which Thomson opened before him, and in this spirit he worked at it
to the last, pouring forth song after song almost to his
latest breath.   Hardly less interesting than the songs themselves, which from time to time he sent to Thomson, were
the letters with which he accompanied them.   In these his
judgment and critical power are as conspicuous as his genius and his enthusiasm for the native melodies.   For all
who take interest in songs and in the laws which govern

their movement, I know not where else they would find
hints so valuable as in these occasional remarks on his own
and others' songs, by the greatest lyric singer whom the
modern world has seen.

The bard who furnished the English songs for this collection was a certain Dr. Wolcot, known as Peter Pindar.
This poetizer, who seems to have been wholly devoid of
genius, but to have possessed a certain talent for hitting
the taste of the hour, was then held in high esteem; he
has long since been forgotten. Even Burns speaks of him
with much respect. "The very name of Peter Pindar is
an acquisition to your work," he writes to Thomson. Well
might Chambers say, "It is a humiliating thought that Peter Pindar was richly pensioned by the booksellers, while
Burns, the true sweet singer, lived in comparative poverty." Hard measure has been dealt to Thomson for not having liberally remunerated Burns for the priceless treasures
which he supplied to the Collection. Chambers and others, who have thoroughly examined the whole matter, have
shown this censure to be undeserved. Thomson himself
was by no means rich, and his work brought him nothing
but outlay as long as Burns lived. Indeed once, in July,
1793, when Thomson had sent Burns some money in return for his songs, the bard thus replied:

"I assure you, my dear sir, that you truly hurt me with
your pecuniary parcel. It degrades me in my own eyes.
However, to return it would savour of affectation; but,
as to any more traffic of that debtor and creditor kind, I
swear, by that honour which crowns the upright statue
of *Robert Burns's Integrity*, on the least motion of it, I
will indignantly spurn the by-pact transaction, and from
that moment commence entire stranger to you. Burns's
character for generosity of sentiment and independence of

mind will, I trust, long outlive any of his wants which the
cold, unfeeling ore can supply; at least I will take care
that such a character he shall deserve."

This sentiment was no doubt inconsistent, and may be
deemed Quixotic, when we remember that for his poems
Burns was quite willing to accept all that Creech would
offer. Yet one cannot but honour it. He felt that both
Johnson and Thomson were enthusiasts, labouring to em-
balm in a permanent form their country's minstrelsy, and
that they were doing this without any hope of profit. He
too would bear his part in the noble work; if he had not
in other respects done full justice to his great gifts, in this
way he would repay some of the debt he owed to his
country, by throwing into her national melodies the whole
wealth and glory of his genius. And this he would do,
"all for love, and nothing for reward." And the continual effort to do this worthily was the chief relaxation
and delight of those sad later years. When he died, he
had contributed to Thomson's work sixty songs, but of
these only six had then appeared, as only one half-volume
of Thomson's work had then been published. Burns
had given Thomson the copyright of all the sixty songs;
but as soon as a posthumous edition of the poet's works
was proposed, Thomson returned all the songs to the
poet's family, to be included in the forthcoming edition,
along with the interesting letters which had accompanied
the songs. Thomson's collection was not completed till
1841, when the sixth and last volume of it appeared. It
is affecting to know that Thomson himself, who was older
than Burns by two years, survived him for more than five-
and-fifty, and died in February, 1851, at the ripe old age
of ninety-four.

CHAPTER VII.

LAST YEARS.

DURING those Dumfries years little is to be done by the biographer but to trace the several incidents in Burns's quarrel with the world, his growing exasperation, and the evil effects of it on his conduct and his fortunes. It is a painful record, but since it must be given, it shall be with as much brevity as is consistent with truth.

In July, 1793, Burns made an excursion into Galloway, accompanied by a Mr. Syme, who belonging, like himself, to the Excise, admired the poet, and agreed with his politics. Syme has preserved a record of this journey, and the main impression left by the perusal of it is the strange access of ill-temper which had come over Burns, who kept venting his spleen in epigrams on all whom he disliked, high and low. They visited Kenmure, where lived Mr. Gordon, the representative of the old Lords Kenmure. They passed thence over the muirs to Gatehouse, in a wild storm, during which Burns was silent, and crooning to himself what, Syme says, was the first thought of *Scots wha hae*. They were engaged to go to St. Mary's Isle, the seat of the Earl of Selkirk; but Burns was in such a savage mood against all lords, that he was with difficulty persuaded to go thither, though Lord Selkirk was no Tory, but a Whig, like himself, and the father of his old friend, Lord Daer, by this time deceased, who had first convinced him that a lord might possibly be an honest and kind-hearted man. When they were once under the hospitable roof of St. Mary's Isle, the kindness with which they were received appeased the poet's bitterness. The Earl was benign, the young ladies were beautiful, and two of them sang Scottish songs charmingly. Urbani, an Italian musician who had edited Scotch music, was there, and sang many Scottish melodies, accompanying them with instrumental music. Burns recited some of his songs amid the deep silence that is most expressive of admiration. The evening passed very pleasantly, and the lion of the morning had, ere the evening was over, melted to a lamb.

Scots wha hae has been mentioned. Mr. Syme tells us that it was composed partly while Burns was riding in a storm between Gatehouse and Kenmure, and partly on the second morning after this, when they were journeying from St. Mary's Isle to Dumfries. And Mr. Syme adds that next day the poet presented him with one copy of the poem for himself, and a second for Mr. Dalzell. Mr. Carlyle says, "This Dithyrambic was composed on horseback; in riding in the middle of tempests over the wildest Galloway moor, in company with a Mr. Syme, who, observing the poet's looks, forbore to speak—judiciously enough—for a man composing Bruce's address might be unsafe to trifle with. Doubtless this stern hymn was singing itself, as he formed it, through the soul of Burns, but to the external ear it should be sung with the throat of the whirlwind."

Burns, however, in a letter to Mr. Thomson, dated September, 1793, gives an account of the composition of his war-ode, which is difficult to reconcile with Mr. Syme's statement. "There is a tradition which I have met with in many places in Scotland," he writes, "that the old air,

Hey, tuttie taitie, was Robert Bruce's march at the battle
of Bannockburn.   This thought, in my yesternight's evening walk, warmed me to a pitch of enthusiasm on the
theme of liberty and independence, which I threw into a
kind of Scottish ode, fitted to the air, that one might suppose to be the gallant royal Scot's address to his heroic
followers on that eventful morning."   He adds that "the
accidental recollection of that glorious struggle for freedom, associated with the glowing ideas of some struggles
of the same nature, *not quite so ancient*, roused my rhyming mania."   So *Bruce's Address* owes its inspiration as
much to Burns's sympathy with the French Republicans
as to his Scottish patriotism.   As to the intrinsic merit of
the ode itself, Mr. Carlyle says, " So long as there is warm
blood in the heart of Scotchmen or man, it will move in
fierce thrills under this war-ode, the best, we believe, that
was ever written by any pen."   To this verdict every son
of Scottish soil is, I suppose, bound to say Amen.   It ought
not, however, to be concealed that there has been a very
different estimate formed of it by judges sufficiently compe-
tent.   I remember to have read somewhere of a conversation between Wordsworth and Mrs. Hemans, in which they
both agreed that the famous ode was not much more than
a commonplace piece of school-boy rhodomontade about
liberty.   Probably it does owe not a little of its power to
the music to which it is sung, and to the associations
which have gathered round it.   The enthusiasm for French
Revolution sentiments, which may have been in Burns's
mind when composing it, has had nothing to do with the
delight with which thousands since have sung and listened
to it.   The poet, however, when he first conceived it, was
no doubt raging inwardly, like a lion, not only caged, but
muzzled with the gag of his servitude to Government.

But for this, what diatribes in favour of the Revolution might we not have had, and what pain must it have been to Burns to suppress these under the coercion of external authority! Partly to this feeling, as well as to other causes, may be ascribed such outbursts as the following, written to a female correspondent, immediately after his return from the Galloway tour:

"There is not among all the martyrologies that ever were penned, so rueful a narrative as the lives of the poets. In the comparative view of wretches, the criterion is not what they are doomed to suffer, but how they are formed to bear. Take a being of our kind, give him a stronger imagination, and a more delicate sensibility, which between them will ever engender a more ungovernable set of passions than are the usual lot of man; implant in him an irresistible impulse to some idle vagary, . . . in short, send him adrift after some pursuit which shall eternally mislead him from the paths of lucre, and yet curse him with a keener relish than any man living for the pleasures that lucre can purchase; lastly, fill up the measure of his woes by bestowing on him a spurning sense of his own dignity—and you have created a wight nearly as miserable as a poet." This passage will recall to many the catalogue of sore evils to which poets are by their temperament exposed, which Wordsworth in his *Leech-gatherer* enumerates.

> "The fear that kills,
> And hope that is unwilling to be fed;
> Cold, pain, and labour, and all fleshly ills;
> And mighty poets in their misery dead."

In writing that poem Wordsworth had Burns among others prominently in his eye. What a commentary is the life of the more impulsive poet on the lines of his

younger and more self-controlling brother! During those
years of political unrest and of growing mental disquiet,
his chief solace was, as I have said, to compose songs for
Thomson's Collection, into which he poured a continual
supply. Indeed it is wonderful how often he was able to
escape from his own vexations into that serener atmosphere,
and there to suit melodies and moods most alien to his
own with fitting words.

Here in one of his letters to Thomson is the way he describes himself in the act of composition. "My way is—
I consider the poetic sentiment correspondent to my idea
of the musical expression; then choose my theme; begin
one stanza; when that is composed, which is generally the
most difficult part of the business, I walk out, sit down
now and then, look out for objects in nature around me
that are in unison and harmony with the cogitations of
my fancy and workings of my bosom; humming every
now and then the air with the verses I have framed.
When I feel my Muse beginning to jade, I retire to the
solitary fireside of my study, and there commit my effusions to paper; swinging at intervals on the hind legs of
my elbow-chair, by way of calling forth my own critical
strictures as my pen goes on." To this may be added
what Allan Cunningham tells us. "While he lived in
Dumfries he had three favourite walks — on the Dock-
green by the river-side; among the ruins of Lincluden
College; and towards the Martingdon-ford, on the north
side of the Nith. This latter place was secluded, com-
manded a view of the distant hills and the romantic tow-
ers of Lincluden, and afforded soft greensward banks to
rest upon, within sight and sound of the stream. As soon
as he was heard to hum to himself, his wife saw that he
had something in his mind, and was prepared to see him

snatch up his hat, and set silently off for his musing-ground. 'When by himself, and in the open air, his ideas arranged themselves in their natural order — words came at will, and he seldom returned without having finished a song. . . . When the verses were finished, he passed them' through the ordeal of Mrs. Burns's voice, listened attentively when she sang; asked her if any of the words were difficult; and when one happened to be too rough, he readily found a smoother; but he never, save at the resolute entreaty of a scientific musician, sacrificed sense to sound. The autumn was his favourite season, and the twilight his favourite hour of study."

Regret has often been expressed that Burns spent so much time and thought on writing his songs, and, in this way, diverted his energies from higher aims. Sir Walter has said, "Notwithstanding the spirit of many of his lyrics, and the exquisite sweetness and simplicity of others, we cannot but deeply regret that so much of his time and talents was frittered away in compiling and composing for musical collections. There is sufficient evidence that even the genius of Burns could not support him in the monotonous task of writing love-verses, on heaving bosoms and sparkling eyes, and twisting them into such rhythmical forms as might suit the capricious evolutions of Scotch reels and strathspeys." Even if Burns, instead of continual song-writing during the last eight years of his life, had concentrated his strength on "his grand plan of a dramatic composition" on the subject of Bruce's adventures, it may be doubted whether he would have done so much to enrich his country's literature as he has done by the songs he composed. But considering how desultory his habits became, if Johnson and Thomson had not, as it were, set him a congenial task, he might not have produced anything at all during those years. There is, however, another aspect in which the continual composition of love-ditties must be regretted. The few genuine love-songs, straight from the heart, which he composed, such as *Of a' the Airts*, *To Mary in Heaven*, *Ye Banks and Braes*, can hardly be too highly prized. But there are many others, which arose from a lower and fictitious source of inspiration. He himself tells Thomson that when he wished to compose a love-song, his recipe was to put himself on a "regimen of admiring a beautiful woman." This was a dangerous regimen, and when it came to be often repeated, as it was, it cannot have tended to his peace of heart, or to the purity of his life.

The first half of the year 1794 was a more than usually unhappy time with Burns. It was almost entirely songless. Instead of poetry, we hear of political dissatisfaction, excessive drinking-bouts, quarrels, and self-reproach. This was the time when our country was at war with the French Republic—a war which Burns bitterly disliked, but his employment under Government forced him to set "a seal on his lips as to those unlucky politics." A regiment of soldiers was quartered in the town of Dumfries, and to Burns's eye the sight of their red coats was so offensive, that he would not go down the plainstones lest he should meet "the epauletted puppies," who thronged the street. One of these epauletted puppies, whom he so disliked, found occasion to pull Burns up rather smartly. The poet, when in his cups, had in the hearing of a certain captain proposed as a toast, "May our success in the present war be equal to the justice of our cause." The soldier called him to account—a duel seemed imminent, and Burns had next day to write an apologetic letter, in order to avoid the risk of ruin. About the same time he was

involved, through intemperance, in another and more painful quarrel. It has been already noticed that at Woodley Park he was a continual guest. With Mrs. Riddel,
who was both beautiful and witty, he carried on a kind of
poetic flirtation. Mr. Walter Riddel, the host, was wont
to press his guests to deeper potations than were usual
even in those hard-drinking days. One evening, when the
guests had sat till they were inflamed with wine, they entered the drawing-room, and Burns in some way grossly
insulted the fair hostess. Next day he wrote a letter of
the most abject and extravagant penitence. This, however, Mr. and Mrs. Riddel did not think fit to accept.
Stung by this rebuff, Burns recoiled at once to the opposite extreme of feeling, and penned a grossly scurrilous
monody on "a lady famed for her caprice." This he followed up by other lampoons, full of "coarse rancour
against a lady who had showed him many kindnesses."
The Laird of Friars Carse and his lady naturally sided
with their relatives, and grew cold to their old friend of
Ellisland. While this coldness lasted, Mr. Riddel, of Friars
Carse, died in the spring-time, and the poet, remembering
his friend's worth and former kindness, wrote a sonnet
over him—not one of his best or most natural performances, yet showing the return of his better heart. During
the same spring we hear of Burns going to the house of
one of the neighbouring gentry, and dining there, not with
the rest of the party, but, by his own choice, it would
seem, with the housekeeper in her room, and joining the
gentlemen in the dining-room after the ladies had retired.
He was now, it seems, more disliked by ladies than by
men — a change since those Edinburgh days, when the
highest dames of the land had spoken so rapturously of
the charm of his conversation.

Amid the gloom of this unhappy time (1791), Burns turned to his old Edinburgh friend, Alexander Cunningham, and poured forth this passionate and well-known complaint:—" Canst thou minister to a mind diseased? Canst thou speak peace and rest to a soul tossed on a sea of troubles, without one friendly star to guide her course, and dreading that the next surge may overwhelm her? Of late, a number of domestic vexations, and some pecuniary share in the ruin of these cursed times—losses which, though trifling, were what I could ill bear—have so irritated me, that my feelings at times could only be envied by a reprobate spirit listening to the sentence that dooms it to perdition.—Are you deep in the language of consolation? I have exhausted in reflection every topic of comfort. A heart at ease would have been charmed with my sentiments and reasonings; but as to myself, I was like Judas Iscariot preaching the Gospel. . . . Still there are two great pillars that bear us up amid the wreck of misfortune and misery. The one is composed of a certain noble, stubborn something in man, known by the names of Courage, Fortitude, Magnanimity. The other is made up of those feelings and sentiments which, however the sceptic may deny them, or the enthusiast may disfigure them, are yet, I am convinced, original and component parts of the human soul, those senses of the mind—if I may be allowed the expression—which connect us with and link us to those awful obscure realities—an all-powerful and equally beneficent God, and a world to come, beyond death and the grave. The first gives the nerve of combat, while a ray of hope beams on the field: the last pours the balm of comfort into the wounds which time can never cure."

This remarkable, or, as Lockhart calls it, noble letter,

was written on February 25, 1794. It was probably a few
months later, perhaps in May of the same year, while
Burns was still under this depression, that there occurred
an affecting incident, which has been preserved by Lockhart. Mr. David McCulloch, of Ardwell, told Lockhart,
"that he was seldom more grieved than when, riding into
Dumfries one fine summer's evening, to attend a country
ball, he saw Burns walking alone, on the shady side of the
principal street of the town, while the opposite part was
gay with successive groups of gentlemen and ladies, all
drawn together for the festivities of the night, not one of
whom seemed willing to recognize the poet. The horse-
man dismounted and joined Burns, who, on his propos-
ing to him to cross the street, said, 'Nay, nay, my young
friend, that's all over now;' and quoted, after a pause, some
verses of Lady Grizzell Baillie's pathetic ballad:

> "'His bonnet stood ance fu' fair on his brow,
>   His auld ane looked better than mony ane's new;
>   But now he lets 't wear ony way it will hing,
>   And casts himsell dowie upon the corn-bing.
>
> "'O, were we young, as we ance hae been,
>   We suld hae been galloping down on yon green,
>   And linking it owre the lily-white lea—
>   And werena my heart light, I wad die.'"

"It was little in Burns's character to let his feelings on
certain subjects escape in this fashion. He immediately
after citing these verses assumed the sprightliness of his
most pleasing manner; and taking his young friend home
with him, entertained him very agreeably until the hour
of the ball arrived, with a bowl of his usual potation, and
Bonnie Jean's singing of some verses which he had recently composed."

In June we find him expressing to Mrs. Dunlop the earliest hint that he felt his health declining. "I am afraid," he says, "that I am about to suffer for the follies of my youth. My medical friends threaten me with flying gout; but I trust they are mistaken." And again, a few months later, we find him, when writing to the same friend, recurring to the same apprehensions. Vexation and disappointment within, and excesses, if not continual, yet too frequent, from without, had for long been undermining his naturally strong but nervously sensitive frame, and those symptoms were now making themselves felt, which were soon to lay him in an early grave. As the autumn drew on, his singing powers revived, and till the close of the year he kept pouring into Thomson a stream of songs, some of the highest stamp, and hardly one without a touch such as only the genuine singer can give.

The letters, too, to Thomson, with which he accompanies his gifts, are full of suggestive thoughts on song, hints most precious to all who care for such matters. For the forgotten singers of his native land he is full of sympathy. "By the way," he writes to Thomson, "are you not vexed to think that those men of genius, for such they certainly were, who composed our fine Scottish lyrics, should be unknown?"

Many of the songs of that autumn were, as usual, love-ditties; but when the poet could forget the lint-white locks of Chloris, of which kind of stuff there is more than enough, he would write as good songs on other and manlier subjects. Two of these, written, the one in November, 1794, the other in January, 1795, belong to the latter order, and are worthy of careful regard, not only for their excellence as songs, but also as illustrations of the poet's mood of mind at the time when he composed them.

The first is this—

> "Contented wi' little, and cantie wi' mair,
>   Whene'er I forgather wi' sorrow and care,
>   I gie them a skelp as they're creepin' alang,
>   Wi' a cog o' gude swats, and an auld Scottish sang.
>
> ♪ I whyles claw the elbow o' troublesome thought;
>   But man is a soger, and life is a faught:
>   My mirth and gude humour are coin in my pouch,
>   And my Freedom's my lairdship nae monarch dare touch.
>
> "A towmond o' trouble, should that be my fa',
>   A night o' gude fellowship sowthers it a';
>   When at the blythe end o' our journey at last,
>   Wha the deil ever thinks o' the road he has past?
>
> "Blind Chance, let her snapper and stoyte on her way;
>   Be't to me, be't frae me, e'en let the jade gae:
>   Come Ease, or come Travail, come Pleasure or Pain,
>   My warst word is—Welcome, and welcome again."

This song gives Burns's idea of himself, and of his struggle with the world, when he could look on both from the placid, rather than the despondent side. He regarded it as a true picture of himself; for, when a good miniature of him had been done, he wrote to Thomson that he wished a vignette from it to be prefixed to this song, that, in his own words, "the portrait of my face and the picture of my mind may go down the stream of time together." Burns had more moods of mind than most men, and this was, we may hope, no unfrequent one with him. But if we would reach the truth, we probably ought to strike a balance between the spirit of this song and the dark moods depicted in some of those letters already quoted.

The other song of the same time is the well-known *A Man's a Man for a' that.* This powerful song speaks out

in his best style a sentiment that through all his life had
been dear to the heart of Burns. It has been quoted, they
say, by Béranger in France, and by Goethe in Germany,
and is the word which springs up in the mind of all for-
eigners when they think of Burns. It was inspired, no
doubt, by his keen sense of social oppression, quickened
to white heat by influences that had lately come from
France, and by what he had suffered for his sympathy
with that cause. It has since become the watchword of
all who fancy that they have secured less, and others more,
of this world's goods than their respective merit deserves.
Stronger words he never wrote.

> "The rank is but the guinea's stamp,
>   The man's the gowd for a' that."

That is a word for all time. Yet perhaps it might have
been wished that so noble a song had not been marred by
any touch of social bitterness. A lord, no doubt, may be
a "birkie" and a "coof," but may not a ploughman be
so too ? This great song Burns wrote on the first day of
1795.

   Towards the end of 1794, and in the opening of 1795,
the panic which had filled the land in 1792, from the doings of the French republicans, and their sympathizers in
this country, began to abate ; and the blast of Government
displeasure, which for a time had beaten heavily on Burns,
seemed to have blown over. He writes to Mrs. Dunlop on
the 29th of December, 1794, " My political sins seem to be
forgiven me ;" and as a proof of it he mentions that during the illness of his superior officer, he had been appointed to act as supervisor—a duty which he discharged for
about two months. In the same letter he sends to that
good lady his usual kindly greeting for the coming year,

and concludes thus:—"What a transient business is life!
Very lately I was a boy; but t' other day I was a young
man; and I already begin to feel the rigid fibre and stiff-
ening joints of old age coming fast o'er my frame. With
all the follies of youth, and, I fear, a few vices of manhood, still I congratulate myself on having had, in early
days, religion strongly impressed on my mind." Burns always keeps his most serious thoughts for this good lady.
Herself religious, she no doubt tried to keep the truths
of religion before the poet's mind. And he naturally was
drawn out to reply in a tone more unreserved than when
he wrote to most others.

In February of the ensuing year, 1795, his duties as supervisor led him to what he describes as the "unfortunate,
wicked little village" of Ecclefechan, in Annandale. The
night after he arrived, there fell the heaviest snow-storm
known in Scotland within living memory. When people
awoke next morning they found the snow up to the windows of the second story of their houses. In the hollow
of Campsie hills it lay to the depth of from eighty to a
hundred feet, and it had not disappeared from the streets
of Edinburgh on the king's birthday, the 4th of June.
Storm-stayed at Ecclefechan, Burns indulged in deep potations and in song-writing. Probably he imputed to the
place that with which his own conscience reproached himself. Currie, who was a native of Ecclefechan, much of-
fended, says, "The poet must have been tipsy indeed to
abuse sweet Ecclefechan at this rate." It was also the
birthplace of the poet's friend Nicol, and of a greater than
he. On the 4th of December in the very year on which
Burns visited it, Mr. Thomas Carlyle was born in that village. Shortly after his visit, the poet beat his brains to
find a rhyme for Ecclefechan, and to twist it into a song.

In March of the same year we find him again joining in
local politics, and writing electioneering ballads for Heron
of Heron, the Whig candidate for the Stewartry of Kirkcudbright, against the nominee of the Earl of Galloway,
against whom and his family Burns seems to have har-
boured some peculiar enmity.

Mr. Heron won the election, and Burns wrote to him
about his own prospects:—"The moment I am appointed
supervisor, in the common routine I may be nominated on
the collectors' list; and this is always a business of purely political patronage. A collectorship varies much, from
better than 200*l.* to near 1000*l.* a year. A life of literary
leisure, with a decent competency, is the summit of my
wishes."

The hope here expressed was not destined to be fulfilled.
It required some years for its realization, and the years allotted to Burns were now nearly numbered. The prospect
which he here dwells on may, however, have helped to
lighten his mental gloom during the last year of his life.
For one year of activity there certainly was, between the
time when the cloud of political displeasure against him
disappeared towards the end of 1794, and the time when
his health finally gave way in the autumn of 1795, during
which, to judge by his letters, he indulged much less in
outbursts of social discontent. One proof of this is seen
in the following fact. In the spring of 1795, a volunteer
corps was raised in Dumfries, to defend the country, while
the regular army was engaged abroad, in war with France.
Many of the Dumfries Whigs, and among them Burns's
friends, Syme and Dr. Maxwell, enrolled themselves in the
corps, in order to prove their loyalty and patriotism, on
which some suspicions had previously been cast. Burns
too offered himself, and was received into the corps. Al-

lan Cunningham remembered the appearance of the regiment, "their odd but not ungraceful dress; white kerseymere breeches and waistcoat; short blue coat, faced with red; and round hat, surmounted by a bearskin, like the helmets of the Horse Guards." He remembered the poet too, as he showed among them, "his very swarthy face, his ploughman stoop, his large dark eyes, and his awkwardness in handling his arms." But if he could not handle his musket deftly, he could do what none else in that or any other corps could, he could sing a patriotic stave which thrilled the hearts not only of his comrades, but every Briton from Land's End to Johnny Groat's.

This is one of the verses:—

> "The kettle o' the kirk and state
>   Perhaps a clout may fail in't;
> But deil a foreign tinkler loun
>   Shall ever ca' a nail in't.
> Our fathers' blude the kettle bought,
>   And wha wad dare to spoil it?
> By heavens! the sacrilegious dog
>   Shall fuel be to boil it!
> By heavens! the sacrilegious dog
>   Shall fuel be to boil it!"

This song flew throughout the land, hit the taste of the country-people everywhere, and is said to have done much to change the feelings of those who were disaffected. Much blame has been cast upon the Tory Ministry, then in power, for not having offered a pension to Burns. It was not, it is said, that they did not know of him, or that they disregarded his existence. For Mr. Addington, afterwards Lord Sidmouth, we have seen, deeply felt his genius, acknowledged it in verse, and is said to have urged his claims upon the Government. Mr. Pitt, soon after the po-

et's death, is reported to have said of Burns's poetry, at
the table of Lord Liverpool, " I can think of no verse since
Shakespeare's that has so much the appearance of coming
sweetly from nature." It is on Mr. Dundas, however, at
that time one of the Ministry, and the autocrat of all Scottish affairs, that the heaviest weight of blame has fallen.
But perhaps this is not altogether deserved. There is the
greatest difference between a literary man, who holds his
political opinions in private, but refrains from mingling
in party politics, and one who zealously espouses one side,
and employs his literary power in promoting it. He
threw himself into every electioneering business with his
whole heart, wrote, while he might have been better employed, electioneering ballads of little merit, in which he
lauded Whig men and theories, and lampooned, often scur-
rilously, the supporters of Dundas. No doubt it would
have been magnanimous in the men then in power to have
overlooked all these things, and, condoning the politics,
to have rewarded the poetry of Burns. And it were to be
wished that such magnanimity were more common among
public men. But we do not see it practised even at the
present day, any more than it was in the time of Burns.

During the first half of 1795 the poet had gone on with
his accustomed duties, and, during the intervals of business, kept sending to Thomson the songs he from time to
time composed.

His professional prospects seemed at this time to be
brightening, for about the middle of May, 1795, his
staunch friend, Mr. Graham, of Fintray, would seem to
have revived an earlier project of having him transferred
to a post in Leith, with easy duty and an income of nearly
200*l.* a year. This project could not at the time be carried out; but that it should have been thought of proves

8*

that political offences of the past were beginning to be
forgotten. During this same year there were symptoms
that the respectable persons who had for some time frown-
ed on him were willing to relent. A combination of causes,
his politics, the Riddel quarrel, and his own many imprudences, had kept him under a cloud. And this disfavour
of the well-to-do had not increased his self-respect or made
him more careful about the company he kept. Disgust
with the world had made him reckless and defiant. But
with the opening of 1795, the Riddels were reconciled to
him, and received him once more into their good graces;
and others, their friends, probably followed their example.

But the time was drawing near when the smiles or the
frowns of the Dumfries magnates would be alike indiffer-
ent to him. There has been more than enough of discussion among the biographers of Burns as to how far he
really deteriorated in himself during those Dumfries years,
as to the extent and the causes of the social discredit into
which he fell, and as to the charge that he took to low
company. His early biographers—Currie, Walker, Heron
—drew the picture somewhat darkly; Lockhart and Cunningham have endeavoured to lighten the depth of the
shadows. Chambers has laboured to give the facts impartially, has faithfully placed the lights and the shadows side
by side, and has summed up the whole subject in an ap-
pendix on *The Reputation of Burns in his Later Years*,
to which I would refer any who desire to see this painful subject minutely handled. Whatever extenuations
or excuses may be alleged, all must allow that his course
in Dumfries was on the whole a downward one, and must
concur, however reluctantly, in the conclusion at which
Lockhart, while decrying the severe judgments of Currie,
Heron, and others, is forced by truth to come, that " the

untimely death of Burns was, it is too probable, hastened
by his own intemperances and imprudences." To inquire
minutely, what was the extent of those intemperances, and
what the nature of those imprudences, is a subject which
can little profit any one, and on which one has no heart
to enter. If the general statement of fact be true, the
minute details are better left to the kindly oblivion, which,
but for too prying curiosity, would by this time have over-
taken them.

Dissipated his life for some years certainly had been—
deeply disreputable many asserted it to be. Others, however, there were who took a more lenient view of him.
Findlater, his superior in the Excise, used to assert that
no officer under him was more regular in his public duties.
Mr. Gray, then teacher of Dumfries school, has left it on
record, that no parent he knew watched more carefully
over his children's education—that he had often found the
poet in his home explaining to his eldest boy passages of
the English poets from Shakespeare to Gray, and that the
benefit of the father's instructions was apparent in the
excellence of the son's daily school performances. This
brighter side of the picture, however, is not irreconcilable
with that darker one. For Burns's whole character was
a compound of the most discordant and contradictory elements. Dr. Chambers has well shown that he who at
one hour was the *douce* sober Mr. Burns, in the next was
changed to the maddest of Bacchanals : now he was glowing with the most generous sentiments, now sinking to the
very opposite extreme.

One of the last visits paid to him by any friend from a
distance would seem to have been by Professor Walker,
although the date of it is somewhat uncertain. Eight
years had passed since the Professor had parted with

Burns at Blair Castle, after the poet's happy visit there. In the account which the Professor has left of his two days' interview with Burns at Dumfries, there are traces of disappointment with the change which the intervening years had wrought. It has been alleged that prolonged residence in England had made the Professor fastidious, and more easily shocked with rusticity and coarseness. However this may be, he found Burns, as he thought, not improved, but more dictatorial, more free in his potations, more coarse and gross in his talk, than when he had formerly known him.

For some time past there had not been wanting symptoms to show that the poet's strength was already past its prime. In June, 1794, he had, as we have seen, told Mrs. Dunlop that he had been in poor health, and was afraid he was beginning to suffer for the follies of his youth. His physicians threatened him, he said, with flying gout, but he trusted they were mistaken. In the spring of 1795, he said to one who called on him, that he was beginning to feel as if he were soon to be an old man. Still he went about all his usual employments. But during the latter part of that year his health seems to have suddenly declined. For some considerable time he was confined to a sick-bed. Dr. Currie, who was likely to be well informed, states that this illness lasted from October, 1795, till the following January. No details of his malady are given, and little more is known of his condition at this time, except what he himself has given in a letter to Mrs. Dunlop, and in a rhymed epistle to one of his brother Excisemen.

At the close of the year he must have felt that, owing to his prolonged sickness, his funds were getting low. Else he would not have penned to his friend, Collector Mitchell, the following request:

" Friend of the Poet, tried and leal,
   Wha, wanting thee, might beg or steal ;
Alake, alake, the meikle deil
      Wi' a' his witches
Are at it, skelpin' ! jig and reel,
      In my poor pouches.

" I modestly fu fain wad hint it,
   That one pound one, I sairly want it ;
If wi' the hizzie down ye sent it,
      It would be kind ;
And while my heart wi' life-blood dunted,
      I'd bear't in mind.

     *   *   *   *   *

" POSTSCRIPT.

" Ye've heard this while how I've been licket,
   And by fell death was nearly nicket :
Grim loun ! he gat me by the fecket,
      And sair me sheuk ;
But by gude luck I lap a wicket,
      And turn'd a neuk.

" But by that health, I've got a share o't,
   And by that life, I'm promised mair o't,
My heal and weel I'll take a care o't
      A tentier way :
Then fareweel, folly, hide and hair o't,
      For ance and aye."

It was, alas ! too late now to bid farewell to folly, even
if he could have done so indeed. With the opening of
the year 1796 he somewhat revived, and the prudent resolve of his sickness disappeared with the first prospect of
returning health. Chambers thus records a fact which
the local tradition of Dumfries confirms :—" Early in the
month of January, when his health was in the course of
improvement, Burns tarried to a late hour at a jovial party
in the Globe tavern. Before returning home, he unluckily

remained for some time in the open air, and, overpowered by the effects of the liquor he had drunk, fell asleep. . . . A fatal chill penetrated his bones; he reached home with the seeds of a rheumatic fever already in possession of his weakened frame. In this little accident, and not in the pressure of poverty or disrepute, or wounded feelings or a broken heart, truly lay the determining cause of the sadly shortened days of our national poet."

How long this new access of extreme illness confined him seems uncertain. Currie says for about a week; Chambers surmises a longer time. Mr. Scott Douglas says, that from the close of January till the month of April, he seems to have moved about with some hope of permanent improvement. But if he had such a hope, it was destined not to be fulfilled. Writing on the 31st of January, 1796, to Mrs. Dunlop, the trusted friend of so many confidences, this is the account he gives of himself:

"I have lately drunk deep of the cup of affliction. The autumn robbed me of my only daughter and darling child, and that at a distance, too, and so rapidly as to put it out of my power to pay the last duties to her. I had scarcely begun to recover from that shock, when I became myself the victim of a most severe rheumatic fever, and long the die spun doubtful; until, after many weeks of a sick-bed, it seems to have turned up life, and I am beginning to crawl across my room, and once indeed have been before my own door in the street." In these words Burns would seem to have put his two attacks together, as though they were but one prolonged illness.

It was about this time that, happening to meet a neighbour in the street, the poet talked with her seriously of his health, and said among other things this : " I find that a man may live like a fool, but he will scarcely die like one." As from time to time he appeared on the street during the early months of 1796, others of his old acquaintance were struck by the sight of a tall man of slovenly appearance and sickly aspect, whom a second look showed to be Burns, and that he was dying. Yet in that February there were still some flutters of song, one of which was, *Hey for the Lass wi' a Tocher*, written in answer to Thomson's beseeching inquiry if he was never to hear from him again. Another was a rhymed epistle, in which he answers the inquiries of the colonel of his Volunteer Corps after his health.

From about the middle of April, Burns seldom left his room, and for a great part of each day was confined to bed. May came — a beautiful May — and it was hoped that its genial influences might revive him. But while young Jeffrey was writing, " It is the finest weather in the world—the whole country is covered with green and blossoms ; and the sun shines perpetually through a light east wind," Burns was shivering at every breath of the breeze. At this crisis his faithful wife was laid aside, unable to attend him. But a young neighbour, Jessie Lewars, sister of a brother exciseman, came to their house, assisted in all household work, and ministered to the dying poet. She was at this time only a girl, but she lived to be a wife and mother, and to see an honoured old age. Whenever we think of the last days of the poet, it is well to remember one who did so much to smooth his dying pillow.

Burns himself was deeply grateful, and his gratitude as usual found vent in song. But the old manner still clung to him. Even then he could not express his gratitude to his young benefactress without assuming the tone of a fancied lover. Two songs in this strain he addressed to Jessie Lewars. Of the second of these it is told, that one

morning the poet said to her that if she would play to
him any favourite tune for which she desired to have new
words, he would do his best to meet her wish. She sat
down at the piano, and played over several times the air
of an old song beginning thus:

> "The robin cam to the wren's nest,
>   And keekit in, and keekit in."

As soon as Burns had taken in the melody, he set to,
and in a few minutes composed these beautiful words, the
second of the songs which he addressed to Jessie:

> "Oh! wert thou in the cauld blast,
>   On yonder lea, on yonder lea,
> My plaidie to the angry airt,
>   I'd shelter thee, I'd shelter thee.
> Or did misfortune's bitter storms
>   Around thee blaw, around thee blaw,
> Thy bield should be my bosom,
>   To share it a', to share it a'.

> "Or were I in the wildest waste,
>   Sae black and bare, sae black and bare,
> The desert were a paradise,
>   If thou wert there, if thou wert there:
> Or were I monarch o' the globe,
>   Wi' thee to reign, wi' thee to reign,
> The brightest jewel in my crown
>   Wad be my queen, wad be my queen."

Mendelssohn is said to have so much admired this song,
that he composed for it what Chambers pronounces an air
of exquisite pathos.

June came, but brought no improvement, rather rapid
decline of health. On the 4th of July (1796) he wrote to
Johnson, "Many a merry meeting this publication (the

Museum) has given us, and possibly it may give us more, though, alas! I fear it. This protracting, slow consuming illness will, I doubt much, my ever dear friend, arrest my sun before he has reached his middle career, and will turn over the poet to far more important concerns than studying the brilliancy of wit or the pathos of sentiment." On the day on which he wrote these words, he left Dumfries for a lonely place called Brow, on the Solway shore, to try the effects of sea-bathing. He went alone, for his wife was unable to accompany him. While he was at Brow, his former friend, Mrs. Walter Riddel, to whom, after their estrangement, he had been reconciled, happened to be staying, for the benefit of her health, in the neighbourhood. She asked Burns to dine with her, and sent her carriage to bring him to her house. This is part of the account she gives of that interview:

" I was struck with his appearance on entering the room. The stamp of death was imprinted on his features. He seemed already touching the brink of eternity. His first salutation was, ' Well, madam, have you any commands for the other world?' I replied that it seemed a doubtful case which of us should be there soonest, and that I hoped he would yet live to write my epitaph. He looked in my face with an air of great kindness, and expressed his concern at seeing me look so ill, with his accustomed sensibility. . . . We had a long and serious conversation about his present situation, and the approaching termination of all his earthly prospects. He spoke of his death without any of the ostentation of philosophy, but with firmness as well as feeling, as an event likely to happen very soon, and which gave him concern chiefly from leaving his four children so young and unprotected, and his wife hourly expecting a fifth. He mentioned, with seeming pride and

satisfaction, the promising genius of his eldest son, and
the flattering marks of approbation he had received from
his teachers, and dwelt particularly on his hopes of that
boy's future conduct and merit.   His anxiety for his family seemed to hang heavy on him, and the more perhaps
from the reflection that he had not done them all the justice he was so well qualified to do.   Passing from this
subject, he showed great concern about the care of his literary fame, and particularly the publication of his posthumous works.   He said he was well aware that his death
would create some noise, and that every scrap of his writing would be revived against him to the injury of his future reputation ; that his letters and verses written with
unguarded and improper freedom, and which he earnest-
ly wished to have buried in oblivion, would be handed
about by idle vanity or malevolence, when no dread of
his resentment would restrain them, or prevent the cen-
sures of shrill-tongued malice, or the insidious sarcasms
of envy, from pouring forth all their venom to blast his
fame.

"He lamented that he had written many epigrams on
persons against whom he entertained no enmity, and whose
characters he would be sorry to wound ; and many indif-
ferent poetical pieces, which he feared would now, with all
their imperfections on their head, be thrust upon the world.
On this account he deeply regretted having deferred to put
his papers in a state of arrangement, as he was now incapable of the exertion. . . . The conversation," she adds,
"was kept up with great evenness and animation on his
side.   I had seldom seen his mind greater or more collected.   There was frequently a considerable degree of vivacity
in his sallies, and they would probably have had a greater
share, had not the concern and dejection I could not dis-

guise damped the spirit of pleasantry he seemed not un-
willing to indulge.

"We parted about sunset on the evening of that day
(the 5th July, 1796); the next day I saw him again, and
we parted to meet no more!"

It is not wonderful that Burns should have felt some
anxiety about the literary legacy he was leaving to mankind. Not about his best poems; these, he must have
known, would take care of themselves. Yet even among
the poems which he had published with his name, were
some "which dying" he well might "wish to blot." There
lay among his papers letters too, and other "fallings from
him," which he no doubt would have desired to suppress,
but of which, if they have not all been made public, enough
have appeared to justify his fears of that idle vanity, if not
malevolence, which, after his death, would rake up every
scrap he had written, uncaring how it might injure his
good name, or affect future generations of his admirers.
No poet perhaps has suffered more from the indiscriminate
and unscrupulous curiosity of editors, catering too greedily
for the public, than Burns has done.

Besides anxieties of this kind, he, during those last days,
had to bear another burden of care that pressed even more
closely home. To pain of body, absence from his wife and
children, and haunting anxiety on their account, was added
the pressure of some small debts and the fear of want. By
the rules of the Excise, his full salary would not be allowed
him during his illness; and though the Board agreed to
continue Burns in his full pay, he never knew this in time
to be comforted by it. With his small income diminished,
how could he meet the increased expenditure caused by
sickness? We have seen how at the beginning of the year
he had written to his friend Mitchell to ask the loan of a

guinea.   One or two letters, asking for the payment of
some old debts due to him by a former companion, still
remain.   During his stay at Brow, on the 12th of July, he
wrote to Thomson the following memorable letter:

"After all my boasted independence, curst necessity
compels me to implore you for five pounds.   A cruel
scoundrel of a haberdasher, to whom I owe an account,
taking it into his head that I am dying, has commenced
a process, and will infallibly put me into jail.   Do, for
God's sake, send that sum, and that by return of post.
Forgive me this earnestness, but the horrors of a jail have
made me half distracted.   I do not ask all this gratuitously; for, upon returning health, I hereby promise and en-
gage to furnish you with five pounds' worth of the neatest
song-genius you have seen.   I tried my hand on Rother-
murchie this morning.   The measure is so difficult that it
is impossible to infuse much genius into the lines.   They
are on the other side.   Forgive, forgive me!"   And on
the other side was written Burns's last song, beginning,
"Fairest maid, on Devon banks."   Was it native feeling,
or inveterate habit, that made him that morning revert to
the happier days he had seen on the banks of Devon, and
sing a last song to one of the two beauties he had there
admired?   Chambers thinks it was to Charlotte Hamilton;
the latest editor refers it to Peggy Chalmers.

Thomson at once sent the sum asked for.   He has been
much, but not justly, blamed for not having sent a much
larger sum, and indeed for not having repaid the poet for
his songs long before.   Against such charges it is enough
to reply that when Thomson had formerly volunteered
some money to Burns in return for his songs, the indignant poet told him that if he ever again thought of such
a thing, their intercourse must thenceforth cease.   And

for the smallness of the sum sent, it should be remembered that Thomson was himself a poor man, and had not at this time made anything by his Collection of Songs, and never did make much beyond repayment of his large outlay.

On the same day on which Burns wrote thus to Thomson, he wrote another letter in much the same terms to his cousin, Mr. James Burnes, of Montrose, asking him to assist him with ten pounds, which was at once sent by his relative, who, though not a rich, was a generous-hearted man.

There was still a third letter written on that 12th of July (1796) from Brow. Of Mrs. Dunlop, who had for some months ceased her correspondence with him, the poet takes this affecting farewell:—"I have written you so often, without receiving any answer, that I would not trouble you again but for the circumstances in which I am. An illness which has long hung about me, in all probability will speedily send me beyond that 'bourn whence no traveller returns.' Your friendship, with which for many years you honoured me, was a friendship dearest to my soul. Your conversation, and especially your correspondence, were at once highly entertaining and instructive. With what pleasure did I use to break up the seal! The remembrance yet adds one pulse more to my poor palpitating heart. Farewell!"

On the 14th he wrote to his wife, saying that though the sea-bathing had eased his pains, it had not done anything to restore his health. The following anecdote of him at this time has been preserved:—"A night or two before Burns left Brow, he drank tea with Mrs. Craig, widow of the minister of Ruthwell. His altered appearance excited much silent sympathy; and the evening being beautiful, and the sun shining brightly through the casement, Miss

Craig (afterwards Mrs. Henry Duncan) was afraid the light might be too much for him, and rose to let down the window-blinds. Burns immediately guessed what she meant, and regarding the young lady with a look of great benignity, said, 'Thank you, my dear, for your kind attention; but oh! let him shine: he will not shine long for me.' "

On the 18th July he left Brow, and returned to Dumfries in a small spring-cart. When he alighted, the onlookers saw that he was hardly able to stand, and observed that he walked with tottering steps to his door. Those who saw him enter his house, knew by his appearance that he would never again cross that threshold alive. When the news spread in Dumfries that Burns had returned from Brow and was dying, the whole town was deeply moved. Allan Cunningham, who was present, thus describes what he saw:—" The anxiety of the people, high and low, was very great. Wherever two or three were together, their talk was of Burns, and of him alone. They spoke of his history, of his person, and of his works; of his witty sayings, and sarcastic replies, and of his too early fate, with much enthusiasm, and sometimes with deep feeling. All that he had done, and all that they had hoped he would accomplish, were talked of. Half a dozen of them stopped Dr. Maxwell in the street, and said, 'How is Burns, sir?' He shook his head, saying, 'He cannot be worse,' and passed on to be subjected to similar inquiries farther up the way. I heard one of a group inquire, with much simplicity, 'Who do you think will be our poet now?' "

During the three or four days between his return from Brow and the end, his mind, when not roused by conversation, wandered in delirium. Yet when friends drew near his bed, sallies of his old wit would for a moment return.

To a brother volunteer who came to see him he said, with
a smile, "John, don't let the awkward squad fire over me."
His wife was unable to attend him; and four helpless
children wandered from room to room gazing on their
unhappy parents. All the while, Jessie Lewars was min-
istering to the helpless and to the dying one, and doing
what kindness could do to relieve their suffering. On the
fourth day after his return, the 21st of July, Burns sank
into his last sleep. His children stood around his bed,
and his eldest son remembered long afterwards all the circumstances of that sad hour.

The news that Burns was dead, sounded through all
Scotland like a knell announcing a great national bereave-
ment. Men woke up to feel the greatness of the gift
which in him had been vouchsafed to their generation,
and which had met, on the whole, with so poor a reception. Self-reproach mingled with the universal sorrow, as
men asked themselves whether they might not have done
more to cherish and prolong that rarely gifted life.

Of course there was a great public funeral, in which the
men of Dumfries and the neighbourhood, high and low,
appeared as mourners, and soldiers and volunteers with
colours, muffled drums, and arms reversed, not very appro-
priately mingled in the procession. At the very time
when they were laying her husband in his grave, Mrs.
Burns gave birth to his posthumous son. He was called
Maxwell, after the physician who attended his father, but
he died in infancy. The spot where the poet was laid
was in a corner of St. Michael's churchyard, and the grave
remained for a time unmarked by any monument. After
some years his wife placed over it a plain, unpretending
stone, inscribed with his name and age, and with the names
of his two boys, who were buried in the same place. Well

had it been, if he had been allowed to rest undisturbed in this grave where his family had laid him. But well-meaning, though ignorant, officiousness would not suffer it to be so. Nearly twenty years after the poet's death, a huge, cumbrous, unsightly mausoleum was, by public subscription, erected at a little distance from his original resting-place. This structure was adorned with an ungraceful figure in marble, representing "The muse of Coila finding the poet at the plough, and throwing her inspiring mantle over him." To this was added a long, rambling epitaph in tawdry Latin, as though any inscription which scholars could devise could equal the simple name of Robert Burns. When the new structure was completed, on the 19th September, 1815, his grave was opened, and men for a moment gazed with awe on the form of Burns, seemingly as entire as on the day when first it was laid in the grave. But as soon as they began to raise it, the whole body crumbled to dust, leaving only the head and bones. These relics they bore to the mausoleum which had been prepared for their reception. But not even yet was the poet's dust to be allowed to rest in peace. When his widow died, in March, 1834, the mausoleum was opened, that she might be laid by her husband's side. Some craniologists of Dumfries were then permitted, in the name of so-called science, to desecrate his dust with their inhuman outrage. At the dead of night, between the 31st of March and the 1st of April, these men laid their profane fingers on the skull of Burns, "tried their hats upon it, and found them all too little;" applied their compasses, registered the size of the so-called organs, and "satisfied themselves that Burns had capacity enough to compose *Tam o' Shanter*, *The Cotter's Saturday Night*, and *To Mary in Heaven*." This done, they laid the head once again in the hallowed ground, where, let us hope, it will be disturbed no more. This mausoleum, unsightly though it is, has become a place of pilgrimage whither yearly crowds of travellers resort from the ends of the earth, to gaze on the resting-place of Scotland's peasant poet, and thence to pass to that other consecrated place within ruined Dryburgh, where lies the dust of a kindred spirit by his own Tweed.

9

CHAPTER VIII.

CHARACTER, POEMS, SONGS.

IF this narrative has in any way succeeded in giving the
lights and the shadows of Burns's life, little comment
need now be added. The reader will, it is hoped, gather
from the brief record of facts here presented a better impression of the man as he was, in his strength and in his
weakness, than from any attempt which might have been
made to bring his various qualities together into a moral
portrait. Those who wish to see a comment on his character, at once wise and tender, should turn to Mr. Carlyle's
famous essay on Burns.

What estimate is to be formed of Burns—not as a poet,
but as a man—is a question that will long be asked, and
will be variously answered, according to the principles men
hold, and the temperament they are of. Men of the world
will regard him one way, worshippers of genius in another; and there are many whom the judgments of neither
of these will satisfy. One thing is plain to every one; it
is the contradiction between the noble gifts he had and
the actual life he lived, which make his career the painful
tragedy it was. When, however, we look more closely
into the original outfit of the man, we seem in some sort
to see how this came to be.

Given a being born into the world with a noble nature,

endowments of head and heart beyond any of his time, wide-ranging sympathies, intellectual force of the strongest man, sensibility as of the tenderest woman, possessed also by a keen sense of right and wrong which he had brought from a pure home—place all these high gifts on the one side, and over against them a lower nature, fierce and turbulent, filling him with wild passions which were hard to restrain and fatal to indulge—and between these two opposing natures, a weak and irresolute will, which could overhear the voice of conscience, but had no strength to obey it; launch such a man on such a world as this, and it is but too plain what the end will be. From earliest manhood till the close, flesh and spirit were waging within him interminable war, and who shall say which had the victory? Among his countrymen there are many who are so captivated with his brilliant gifts and his genial temperament, that they will not listen to any hint at the deep defects which marred them. Some would even go so far as to claim honour for him, not only as Scotland's greatest poet, but as one of the best men she has produced. Those who thus try to canonize Burns are no true friends to his memory. They do but challenge the counter-verdict, and force men to recall facts which, if they cannot forget, they would fain leave in silence. These moral defects it is ours to know; it is not ours to judge him who had them.

While some would claim for Burns a niche among Scotland's saints, others would give him rank as one of her religious teachers. This claim, if not so absurd as the other, is hardly more tenable. The religion described by Burns in *The Cotter's Saturday Night* is, it should be remembered, his father's faith, not his own. The fundamental truths of natural religion, faith in God and in immortality, amid sore trials of heart, he no doubt clung to, and has forcibly expressed. But there is nothing in his poems or in his letters which goes beyond sincere deism— nothing which is in any way distinctively Christian.

Even were his teaching of religion much fuller than it is, one essential thing is still wanting. Before men can accept any one as a religious teacher, they not unreasonably expect that his practice should in some measure bear out his teaching. It was not as an authority on such matters that Burns ever regarded himself. In his *Bard's Epitaph*, composed ten years before his death, he took a far truer and humbler measure of himself than any of his critics or panegyrists have done:

> " The poor inhabitant below
>   Was quick to learn and wise to know,
>   And keenly felt the friendly glow
>   And softer flame;
>   But thoughtless folly laid him low,
>   And stained his name.

> " Reader, attend! whether thy soul
>   Soars fancy's flight beyond the pole,
>   Or darkling grubs this earthly hole,
>   In low pursuit;
>   Know, prudent, cautious self-control
>   Is wisdom's root."

"A confession," says Wordsworth, "at once devout, poetical, and human—a history in the shape of a prophecy."

Leaving the details of his personal story, and—

> " Each unquiet theme,
> Where gentlest judgments may misdeem,"

it is a great relief to turn to the bequest that he has left to the world in his poetry. How often has one been tempted to wish that we had known as little of the actual career of Burns as we do of the life of Shakespeare, or even of Homer, and had been left to read his mind and character only by the light of his works! That poetry, though a fragmentary, is still a faithful transcript of what was best in the man; and though his stream of song contains some sediment we could wish away, yet as a whole, how vividly, clearly, sunnily it flows! how far the good preponderates over the evil!

What that good is must now be briefly said. To take his earliest productions first, his poems as distinct from his songs. Almost all the best of these are, with the one notable exception of *Tam O'Shanter*, contained in the Kilmarnock edition. A few pieces actually composed before he went to Edinburgh were included in later editions, but after leaving Mossgiel he never seriously addressed himself to any form of poetry but song-writing. The Kilmarnock volume contains poems descriptive of peasant life and manners, epistles in verse generally to rhyming brethren, a few lyrics on personal feelings, or on incidents like those of the mouse and the daisy, and three songs. In these, the form, the metre, the style and language, even that which is known as Burns's peculiar stanza, all belong to the traditional forms of his country's poetry, and from earlier bards had been handed down to Burns by his two immediate forerunners, Ramsay and Fergusson. To these two he felt himself indebted, and for them he always expresses a somewhat exaggerated admiration. Nothing can more show Burns's inherent power than to compare his poems with even the best of those which he accepted as models. The old framework and metres which his country supplied, he took; asked no other, no better, and into those old bottles poured new wine of his own, and such wine!) What, then, is the peculiar flavour of this new po-

etic wine of Burns's poetry? At the basis of all his power lay absolute truthfulness, intense reality, truthfulness to
the objects which he saw, truthfulness to himself as the
seer of them. This is what Wordsworth recognized as
Burns's leading characteristic. He who acknowledged
few masters, owned Burns as his master in this respect
when he speaks of him—

> "Whose light I hailed when first it shone,
>   And showed my youth,
> How verse may build a princely throne
>   On humble truth."

Here was a man, a son of toil, looking out on the world
from his cottage, on society low and high, and on nature
homely or beautiful, with the clearest eye, the most piercing insight, and the warmest heart; touching life at a
hundred points, seeing to the core all the sterling worth,
nor less the pretence and hollowness of the men he met,
the humour, the drollery, the pathos, and the sorrow of
human existence; and expressing what he saw, not in the
stock phrases of books, but in his own vernacular, the language of his fireside, with a directness, a force, a vitality
that tingled to the finger tips, and forced the phrases of
his peasant dialect into literature, and made them for ever
classical. Large sympathy, generous enthusiasm, reckless
abandonment, fierce indignation, melting compassion, rare
flashes of moral insight, all are there. Everywhere you
see the strong intellect made alive, and driven home to the
mark, by the fervid heart behind it. And if the sight of
the world's inequalities, and some natural repining at his
own obscure lot, mingled from the beginning, as has been
said, " some bitterness of earthly spleen and passion with
the workings of his inspiration, and if these in the end ate

deep into the great heart they had long tormented," who that has not known his experience may venture too strongly to condemn him?

This prevailing truthfulness of nature and of vision manifested itself in many ways. First. In the strength of it, he interpreted the lives, thoughts, feelings, manners of the Scottish peasantry to whom he belonged, as they had never been interpreted before, and never can be again. Take the poem which stands first in the Kilmarnock edition. The Cotter's Dog and the Laird's Dog are, as has been often said, for all their moralizing, true dogs in all their ways. Yet through these, while not ceasing to be dogs, the poet represents the whole contrast between the Cotters' lives, and their Lairds'. This old controversy, which is ever new, between rich and poor, has never been set forth with more humour and power. No doubt it is done from the peasant's point of view. The virtues and hardships of the poor have full justice done to them; the prosperity of the rich, with its accompanying follies and faults, is not spared, perhaps it is exaggerated. The whole is represented with an inimitably graphic hand, and just when the caustic wit is beginning to get too biting, the edge of it is turned by a touch of kindlier humour. The poor dog speaks of

> " Some gentle master,
> Wha, aiblins thrang a-parliamentin,
> For Britain's guid his saul indentin—"

Then Cæsar, the rich man's dog, replies—

> " Haith, lad, ye little ken about it:
> For Britain's guid!—guid faith! I doubt it.
> Say rather, gaun as Premiers lead him,
> An' saying aye or no 's they bid him:

> At operas an' plays parading,
> Mortgaging, gambling, masquerading:
> Or, may be, in a frolic daft,
> To Hague or Calais takes a waft,
> To make a tour an' tak a whirl,
> To learn *bon ton*, an' see the worl'.

> "Then, at Vienna or Versailles,
> He rives his father's auld entails;
> Or by Madrid he takes the rout,
> To thrum guitars and fecht wi' nowt.
>   * * * * * *
> For Britain's guid! for her destruction!
> Wi' dissipation, feud an' faction."

Then exclaims Luath, the poor man's dog—

> "Hech, man! dear sirs! is that the gate
> They waste sae mony a braw estate!
> Are we sae foughten and harass'd
> For gear to gang that gate at last?"

And yet he allows, that for all that

> "—— Thae frank, rantin', ramblin' billies,
> Fient haet o' them's ill-hearted fellows."

"Mark the power of that one word, 'nowt,'" said the late Thomas Aird. "If the poet had said that our young fellows went to Spain to fight with bulls, there would have been some dignity in the thing, but think of his going all that way 'to fecht wi' nowt.' It was felt at once to be ridiculous. That one word conveyed at once a statement of the folly, and a sarcastic rebuke of the folly."

Or turn to the poem of *Halloween.* Here he has sketched the Ayrshire peasantry as they appeared in their hours of merriment—painted with a few vivid strokes a dozen distinct pictures of country lads and lasses, sires and dames, and at the same time preserved for ever the remembrance of antique customs and superstitious observances, which even in Burns's day were beginning to fade, and have now all but disappeared.

Or again, take *The auld Farmer's New-year-morning Salutation to his auld Mare.* In this homely, but most kindly humorous poem, you have the whole toiling life of a ploughman and his horse, done off in two or three touches, and the elements of what may seem a commonplace, but was to Burns a most vivid, experience, are made to live for ever. For a piece of good graphic Scotch, see how he describes the sturdy old mare in the plough setting her face to the furzy braes.

> "Thou never braing't, an' fetch't, and fliskit,
> But thy auld tail thou wad hae whiskit,
> An' spread abreed thy weel-fill'd brisket,
>   Wi' pith an' pow'r,
> Till spritty knowes wad rair't and riskit,
>   An' slypet owre."

To paraphrase this, "Thou didst never fret, or plunge and kick, but thou wouldest have whisked thy old tail, and spread abroad thy large chest, with pith and power, till hillocks, where the earth was filled with tough-rooted plants, would have given forth a cracking sound, and the clods fallen gently over." The latter part of this paraphrase is taken from Chambers. What pure English words could have rendered these things as compactly and graphically?

Of *The Cotter's Saturday Night* it is hardly needful to speak. As a work of art, it is by no means at Burns's highest level. The metre was not native to him. It contains some lines that are feeble, whole stanzas that are

9*

heavy. But as Lockhart has said, in words already quoted, there is none of his poems that does such justice to the better nature that was originally in him. It shows how Burns could reverence the old national piety, however little he may have been able to practise it. It is the more valuable for this, that it is almost the only poem in which either of our two great national poets has described Scottish character on the side of that grave, deep, though undemonstrative reverence, which has been an intrinsic element in it.

No wonder the peasantry of Scotland have loved Burns as perhaps never people loved a poet. He not only sympathized with the wants, the trials, the joys and sorrows of their obscure lot, but he interpreted these to themselves, and interpreted them to others, and this too in their own language, made musical and glorified by genius. He made the poorest ploughman proud of his station and his toil, since Robbie Burns had shared and had sung them. He awoke a sympathy for them in many a heart that otherwise would never have known it. In looking up to him, the Scottish people have seen an impersonation of themselves on a large scale—of themselves, both in their virtues and in their vices.

Secondly. Burns in his poetry was not only the interpreter of Scotland's peasantry, he was the restorer of her nationality. When he appeared, the spirit of Scotland was at a low ebb. The fatigue that followed a century of religious strife, the extinction of her Parliament, the stern suppression of the Jacobite risings, the removal of all symbols of her royalty and nationality, had all but quenched the ancient spirit. Englishmen despised Scotchmen, and Scotchmen seemed ashamed of themselves and of their country. A race of literary men had sprung up in Edinburgh who, as to national feeling, were entirely colourless, Scotchmen in nothing except their dwelling-place. The thing they most dreaded was to be convicted of a Scotticism. Among these learned cosmopolitans in walked Burns, who with the instinct of genius chose for his subject that Scottish life which they ignored, and for his vehicle that vernacular which they despised, and who, touching the springs of long-forgotten emotions, brought back on the hearts of his countrymen a tide of patriotic feeling to which they had long been strangers.

At first it was only his native Ayrshire he hoped to illustrate; to shed upon the streams of Ayr and Doon the power of Yarrow, and Teviot, and Tweed. But his patriotism was not merely local; the traditions of Wallace haunted him like a passion, the wanderings of Bruce he hoped to dramatize. His well-known words about the Thistle have been already quoted. They express what was one of his strongest aspirations. And though he accomplished but a small part of what he once hoped to do, yet we owe it to him first of all that "the old kingdom" has not wholly sunk into a province. If Scotchmen today love and cherish their country with a pride unknown to their ancestors of the last century, if strangers of all countries look on Scotland as a land of romance, this we owe in great measure to Burns, who first turned the tide, which Scott afterwards carried to full flood. All that Scotland had done and suffered, her romantic history, the manhood of her people, the beauty of her scenery, would have disappeared in modern commonplace and manufacturing ugliness, if she had been left without her two "sacred poets."

Thirdly. Burns's sympathies and thoughts were not confined to class nor country; they had something more

catholic in them, they reached to universal man. Few as
were his opportunities of knowing the characters of statesmen and politicians, yet with what "random shots o'
countra wit" did he hit off the public men of his time!
In his address to King George III. on his birthday, how
gay yet caustic is the satire, how trenchant his stroke!
The elder and the younger Pitt, "yon ill-tongued tinkler
Charlie Fox," as he irreverently calls him — if Burns had
sat for years in Parliament, he could scarcely have known
them better. Every one of the Scottish M.P.'s of the
time, from—

> "That slee auld-farran chiel Dundas"

to—

> That glib-gabbit Highland baron
>   The Laird o' Graham,"

and—

> Erskine a spunkie Norlan billie,"

—he has touched their characters as truly as if they had
all been his own familiars. But of his intuitive knowledge
of men of all ranks there is no need to speak, for every
line he writes attests it. Of his fetches of moral wisdom
something has already been said. He would not have
been a Scotchman, if he had not been a moralizer; but
then his moralizings are not platitudes, but truths winged
with wit and wisdom. He had, as we have seen, his limitations—his bias to overvalue one order of qualities, and
to disparage others. Some pleading of his own cause and
that of men of his own temperament, some disparagement
of the severer, less-impulsive virtues, it is easy to discern
in him. Yet, allowing all this, what flashes of moral insight, piercing to the quick! what random sayings flung
forth, that have become proverbs in all lands—"mottoes
of the heart!"

Such are—

> "O wad some Power the giftie gie us,
> To see oursel as ithers see us:
> It wad frae mony a blunder free us,
>   An' foolish notion;"

Or the much-quoted—

> "Facts are chiels that winna ding
>   And downa be disputed;"

Or—

> "The heart ay's the part ay
>   That makes us right or wrang."

Who on the text, "He that is without sin among you, let him first cast a stone," ever preached such a sermon as Burns in his *Address to the unco Guid?* and in his epistle of advice to a young friend, what wisdom! what incisive aphorisms! In passages like these scattered throughout his writings, and in some single poems, he has passed beyond all bonds of place and nationality, and spoken home to the universal human heart.

And here we may note that in that awakening to the sense of human brotherhood, the oneness of human nature, which began towards the end of last century, and which found utterance through Cowper first of the English poets, there has been no voice in literature, then or since, which has proclaimed it more tellingly than Burns. And then his humanity was not confined to man, it overflowed to his lower fellow-creatures. His lines about the pet ewe, the worn-out mare, the field-mouse, the wounded hare, have long been household words. In this tenderness towards animals we see another point of likeness between him and Cowper.

Fourthly. For all aspects of the natural world he has the same clear eye, the same open heart that he has for man. His love of nature is intense, but very simple and

direct, no subtilizings, nor refinings about it, nor any of
that nature-worship which soon after his time came in.
Quite unconsciously, as a child might, he goes into the
outward world for refreshment, for enjoyment, for sympathy. Everywhere in his poetry, nature comes in, not so
much as a being independent of man, but as the background of his pictures of life and human character. How
true his perceptions of her features are, how pure and
transparent the feeling she awakens in him! Take only
two examples. Here is the well-known way he describes
the burn in his *Halloween*—

> "Whyles owre a linn the burnie plays,
>   As thro' the glen it wimpl't ;
> Whyles round a rocky scaur it strays,
>   Whyles in a wiel it dimpl't ;
> Whyles glitter'd to the nightly rays,
>   Wi' bickerin', dancin' dazzle ;
> Whyles cookit underneath the braes,
>   Below the spreading hazel,
>   Unseen that night."

Was ever burn so naturally, yet picturesquely described ?
The next verse can hardly be omitted—

> "Amang the brachens on the brae,
>   Between her an' the moon,
> The deil, or else an outler quey,
>   Gat up an' gae a croon :
> Poor Leezie's heart maist lap the hool ;
>   Near lav'rock height she jumpit ;
> But miss'd a fit, an' in the pool
>   Out-owre the lugs she plumpit,
>   Wi' a plunge that night."

"Maist lap the hool," what condensation in that Scotch
phrase ! The hool is the pod of a pea—poor Lizzie's heart
almost leapt out of its encasing sheath.

Or look at this other picture:

> "Upon a simmer Sunday morn,
>   When Nature's face is fair,
> I walkèd forth to view the corn,
>   And snuff the caller air.
> The risin' sun owre Galston muirs
>   Wi' glorious light was glintin;
> The hares were hirplin down the furrs,
>   The lav'rocks they were chantin
>   Fu' sweet that day."

I have noted only some of the excellences of Burns's poetry, which far outnumber its blemishes. Of these last it is unnecessary to speak; they are too obvious, and whatever is gross, readers can of themselves pass by.

Burns's most considerable poems, as distinct from his songs, were almost all written before he went to Edinburgh. There is, however, one memorable exception. *Tam o' Shanter*, as we have seen, belongs to Ellisland days. Most of his earlier poems were entirely realistic, a transcript of the men and women and scenes he had seen and known, only lifted a very little off the earth, only very slightly idealized. But in *Tam o' Shanter* he had let loose his powers upon the materials of past experiences, and out of them he shaped a tale which was a pure imaginative creation. In no other instance, except perhaps in *The Jolly Beggars*, had he done this; and in that cantata, if the genius is equal, the materials are so coarse, and the sentiment so gross, as to make it, for all its dramatic power, decidedly offensive. It is strange what very opposite judgments have been formed of the intrinsic merit of *Tam o' Shanter*. Mr. Carlyle thinks that it might have been written "all but quite as well by a man, who, in place of genius, had only possessed talent; that it is not so much a poem, as a piece of sparkling rhetoric; the heart of the story still lies hard and dead." On the other hand, Sir Walter Scott has recorded this verdict: "In the inimitable tale of *Tam o' Shanter*, Burns has left us sufficient evidence of his abilities to combine the ludicrous with the awful and even the horrible. No poet, with the exception of Shakespeare, ever possessed the power of exciting the most varied and discordant emotions with such rapid transitions. His humorous description of death in the poem on Dr. Hornbrook, borders on the terrific; and the witches' dance in the Kirk of Alloway is at once ludicrous and horrible." Sir Walter, I believe, is right, and the world has sided with him in his judgment about *Tam o' Shanter*. Nowhere in British literature, out of Shakespeare, is there to be found so much of the power of which Scott speaks — that of combining in rapid transition almost contradictory emotions — if we except perhaps one of Scott's own highest creations, the tale of Wandering Willie, in *Redgauntlet*.

On the songs of Burns a volume might be written, but a few sentences must here suffice. It is in his songs that his soul comes out fullest, freest, brightest; it is as a songwriter that his fame has spread widest, and will longest last. Mr. Carlyle, not in his essay, which does full justice to Burns's songs, but in some more recent work, has said something like this, "Our Scottish son of thunder had, for want of a better, to pour his lightning through the narrow cranny of Scottish song — the narrowest cranny ever vouchsafed to any son of thunder." The narrowest, it may be, but the most effective, if a man desires to come close to his fellow-men, soul to soul. Of all forms of literature the genuine song is the most penetrating, and the most to be remembered; and in this kind Burns is the supreme master. |To make him this, two things combined. First, there was the great background of national melody and antique verse, coming down to him from remote ages, and sounding through his heart from childhood. He was cradled in a very atmosphere of melody, else he never could have sung so well. No one knew better than he did, or would have owned more feelingly, how much he owed to the old forgotten song-writers of his country, dead for ages before he lived, and lying in their unknown graves all Scotland over. From his boyhood he had studied eagerly the old tunes, and the old words where there were such, that had come down to him from the past, treasured every scrap of antique air and verse, conned and crooned them over till he had them by heart. / This was the one form of literature that he had entirely mastered. And from the first he had laid it down as a rule, that the one way to catch the inspiration, and rise to the true fervour of song, was, as he phrased it, "to *sowth* the tune over and over," till the words came spontaneously. /The words of his own songs were inspired by pre-existing tunes, not composed first, and set to music afterwards/ But all this love and study of the ancient songs and outward melody would have gone for nothing, but for the second element, that is the inward melody born in the poet's deepest heart, which received into itself the whole body of national song; and then when it had passed through his soul, sent it forth ennobled and glorified by his own genius.

That which fitted him to do this was the peculiar intensity of his nature, the fervid heart, the trembling sensibility, the headlong passion, all thrilling through an intellect strong and keen beyond that of other men. How mysterious to reflect that the same qualities on their emotional side made him the great songster of the world, and on their practical side drove him to ruin! The first word which Burns composed was a song in praise of his partner on the harvest-rig; the last utterance he breathed in verse was also a song — a faint remembrance of some former affection. Between these two he composed from two to three hundred. It might be wished, perhaps, that he had written fewer, especially fewer love songs; never composed under pressure, and only when his heart was so full he could not help singing. This is the condition on which alone the highest order of songs is born. Probably from thirty to forty songs of Burns could be named which come up to this highest standard. No other Scottish song-writer could show above four or five of the same quality. Of his songs one main characteristic is that their subjects, the substance they lay hold of, belongs to what is most permanent in humanity, those primary affections, those permanent relations of life which cannot change while man's nature is what it is. In this they are wholly unlike those songs which seize on the changing aspects of society. As the phases of social life change, these are forgotten. But no time can superannuate the subjects which Burns has sung; they are rooted in the primary strata, which are steadfast. Then, as the subjects are primary, so the feeling with which Burns regards them is primary too—that is, he gives us the first spontaneous gush—the first throb of his heart, and that a most strong, simple, manly heart. The feeling is not turned over in the reflective faculty, and there artistically shaped—not subtilized and refined away till it has lost its power and freshness; but given at first hand, as it comes warm from within. When he is at his best, you seem to hear the whole song warbling through his spirit, naturally as a bird's. The whole subject is wrapped in an element of music, till it is penetrated and

transfigured by it.   No one else has so much of the native
lilt in him.   When his mind was at the white heat, it is
wonderful how quickly he struck off some of his most perfect songs.   And yet he could, when it was required, go
back upon them, and retouch them line by line, as we saw
him doing in *Ye Banks and Braes*.   In the best of them
the outward form is as perfect as the inward music is all-
pervading, and the two are in complete harmony.

To mention a few instances in which he has given their
ultimate and consummate expression to fundamental human emotions, four songs may be mentioned, in each of
which a different phase of love has been rendered for all
time—

> " Of a' the airts the wind can blaw,"

> " Ye flowery banks o' bonnie Doon,"

> " Go fetch to me a pint o' wine ;"

and that other, in which the calm depth of long-wedded
and happy love utters itself, so blithely yet pathetically—

> " John Anderson, my Jo, John."

Then for comic humour of courtship, there is—

> " Duncan Gray cam here to woo."

For that contented spirit which, while feeling life's troubles, yet keeps " aye a heart aboon them a'," we have—

> "Contented wi' little, and cantie wi' mair."

For friendship rooted in the past, there is—

> " Should auld acquaintance be forgot,"

even if we credit antiquity with some of the verses.

For wild and reckless daring, mingled with a dash of

finer feeling, there is *Macpherson's Farewell*. For patriotic heroism—

> "Scots wha hae wi' Wallace bled;"

and for personal independence, and sturdy, if self-assert-
ing, manhood—

> "A man's a man for a' that."

These are but a few of the many permanent emotions to
which Burns has given such consummate expression, as
will stand for all time.

In no mention of his songs should that be forgotten
which is so greatly to the honour of Burns. He was emphatically the purifier of Scottish song. There are some
poems he has left, there are also a few among his songs,
which we could wish that he had never written. But we
who inherit Scottish song as he left it, can hardly imagine
how much he did to purify and elevate our national melodies. To see what he has done in this way, we have but
to compare Burns's songs with the collection of Scottish
songs published by David Herd, in 1769, a few years before Burns appeared. A genuine poet, who knew well
what he spoke of, the late Thomas Aird, has said, "Those
old Scottish melodies, sweet and strong though they were,
strong and sweet, were, all the more for their very strength
and sweetness, a moral plague, from the indecent words
to which many of them had long been set. How was the
plague to be stayed? All the preachers in the land could
not divorce the grossness from the music. The only way
was to put something better in its stead. This inestimable
something better Burns gave us."

So purified and ennobled by Burns, these songs embody
human emotion in its most condensed and sweetest essence. They appeal to all ranks, they touch all ages, they

cheer toil-worn men under every clime. Wherever the English tongue is heard, beneath the suns of India, amid African deserts, on the western prairies of America, among the squatters of Australia, whenever men of British blood would give vent to their deepest, kindliest, most genial feelings, it is to the songs of Burns they spontaneously turn, and find in them at once a perfect utterance, and a fresh tie of brotherhood. It is this which forms Burns's most enduring claim on the world's gratitude.

THE END.

ENGLISH MEN OF LETTERS.

EDITED BY JOHN MORLEY.

The following Volumes are now ready:

12mo, Cloth, 75 cents per Volume.

Others will be announced.

PUBLISHED BY HARPER & BROTHERS, NEW YORK.

☞ HARPER & BROTHERS *will send any of the above works by mail, postage prepaid, to any part of the United States, on receipt of the price.*

BURNS'S LIFE AND WORKS.

The Life and Works of Robert Burns. Edited by ROBERT CHAMBERS. 4 vols., 12mo, Cloth, $6 00; Half Calf, $13 00.

Mr. Chambers's edition is the completest presentation of the Scottish poet in existence. The various compositions are here strung in strict chronological order upon the Memoir, that they may render up the whole light which they are qualified to throw upon the history of the life and mental progress of Burns, while a new significance is given to them by their being read in connection with the current of events and emotions which led to their production. The result of this plan is not merely a great amount of new biographical detail, but a new sense, efficacy, and feeling in the writings of the poet himself.

All that remains of Burns, the writings he has left, seem to us no more than a poor mutilated fraction of what was in him; brief, broken glimpses of a genius that could never show itself complete; that wanted all things for completeness—culture, leisure, true effort, nay, even length of life. * * * There is something in his poems which forbids the most fastidious student of poetry to pass them by. * * * The excellence of Burns is, indeed, among the *rarest*, whether in poetry or prose; but, at the same time, it is plain, and easily recognized—his indisputable air of truth.—THOMAS CARLYLE.

Burns is by far the greatest poet that ever sprung from the bosom of the people, and lived and died in an humble condition. He was born a poet, if ever man was, and to his native genius alone is owing the perpetuity of his fame. * * * Whatever be the faults or the defects of the poetry of Burns—and no doubt it has many—it has, beyond all that was ever written, this greatest of all merits, intense, life-pervading, and life-breathing truth.—Professor WILSON (*Christopher North*).

PUBLISHED BY HARPER & BROTHERS, NEW YORK.

Sent by mail, postage prepaid, to any part of the United States, on receipt of the price.